HOUSING
WELFARE
LAW

HOUSING WELFARE LAW

by
DAVID TIPLADY, B.A., B. Litt. (Oxon.)
Barrister-at-Law

LONDON
OYEZ PUBLISHING LIMITED
1975

OYEZ PUBLISHING LIMITED
OYEZ HOUSE, 237 LONG LANE
LONDON SE1 4PU
1975

ISBN 85120 262 4

Printed in Great Britain by
Ebenezer Baylis and Son Limited
The Trinity Press, Worcester, and London

PREFACE

Housing law is a complex and far-reaching subject which is developing from day to day. This book deals with only a few of its aspects and is concerned particularly with the problems of those whose housing conditions are inadequate or unsatisfactory. It examines such matters as: the functions of the local authority with regard to housing; the improvement, repair and maintenance of rented property; security of tenure; squatting; harassment and dispossession.

The law governing these matters is often difficult. Frequently the problem is one of complexity and cross-reference. In other areas the law is in an early stage of development, or is in a state of flux, or is simply anachronistic.

I hope that this small work may provide some assistance to those who try to plot a course through the jungle or the scrub.

I have attempted to state the law as at 1st June 1975.

October, 1975 DAVID TIPLADY

CONTENTS

TABLE OF CASES

TABLE OF STATUTES

[*Entries are in alphabetical order.*]

TABLE OF ABBREVIATIONS

C.C.R	County Court Rules
D.H.S.S.	Department of Health and Social Security
D.P.A. 1972	Defective Premises Act 1972
H.A. 1957	Housing Act 1957
H.A. 1961	Housing Act 1961
H.A. 1964	Housing Act 1964
H.A. 1969	Housing Act 1969
H.A. 1974	Housing Act 1974
H.F.A. 1972	Housing Finance Act 1972
L.C.A. 1973	Land Compensation Act 1973
L.P.A. 1925	Law of Property Act 1925
M.C.A. 1973	Matrimonial Causes Act 1973
M.H.A. 1967	Matrimonial Houses Act 1967
N.A.A. 1948	National Assistance Act 1948
O.L.A. 1957	Occupiers' Liability Act 1957
P.H.A. 1936	Public Health Act 1936
P.H.A. 1961	Public Health Act 1961
R.A. 1965	Rent Act 1965
R.A. 1968	Rent Act 1968
R.A. 1974	Rent Act 1974
R.S.C.	Rules of the Supreme Court

CHAPTER 1

THE PROVISION OF HOUSING

The only body under a general legal obligation to provide housing is the local authority. This obligation takes three forms: the duties under Part V of the Housing Act 1957; the duty to rehouse under s.39 of the Land Compensation Act 1973, as amended by the Housing Act 1974; and the duty to provide temporary emergency accommodation under s.21(1)(*b*) of the National Assistance Act 1948, as amended by the Local Government Act 1972.

1. Generally

a. Duties of a Local Authority

It should be noted from the outset that a local authority is under no enforceable *legal* duty to provide housing, whether of a temporary or a permanent kind, simply because a particular person or family happens to want or need it (but see D.H.S.S. Circular no. 18/74, especially paras 8 and 26). The basic duty of a local authority, as laid down in s.91 of the Housing Act 1957, is of a general nature: 'to consider housing conditions in their district and the needs of the district with respect to the provision of further housing accommodation', and, as necessary or when directed, to submit proposals to the central government for the provision of new houses in their area. This duty falls on the district council under s.193(1) of the Local Government Act 1972.

The methods available to a local authority for discharging this general duty are set down in s.92(1):

> A local authority may provide housing accommodation—

(*a*) by the erection of houses on any land acquired or appropriated by them;

(*b*) by the conversion of any buildings into houses;

(*c*) by acquiring houses;

(*d*) by altering, enlarging, repairing or improving any houses or buildings which have, or an estate or interest in which has, been acquired by the local authority.

b. Allocation of Housing

The selection of council house tenants is within the entire discretion of the local authority, which may impose whatever qualifications appear fit, provided that 'reasonable preference is given to persons who are occupying insanitary or over-crowded houses, have large families, or are living under un-satisfactory housing conditions' (s.113(2) H.A.1957).

Many authorities allocate housing on a points basis, although this is not mandatory. Applicants on the housing waiting list are allotted points for various factors, including those specified in s.113(2) and others such as ill health, old age, and length of time spent on the housing waiting list of that or, in some cases, another local authority.

Some authorities, however, (particularly those in the G.L.C. area) will admit applicants to the waiting list only if they satisfy certain initial requirements—for instance that the applicant has resided in the district for a specified minimum period. In *Ealing London Borough Council* v. *Race Relations Board* [1972] A.C. 342 the House of Lords acknowledged the validity of a requirement that the applicant be of British nationality. It is an offence under s.5 (*a*) of the Race Relations Act 1968 to discriminate in housing matters on grounds of *national origin*, i.e. race, but not on grounds of *nationality*, i.e. the country to which political allegiance is owed. The applicant in the *Ealing* case could (and eventually did) qualify to be placed on the housing waiting list by changing his nationality, but national origins, in the sense of race, are immutable.

In addition to the stock of housing held by the housing department of the district council, a limited number of houses is usually available to the social services department; these may be utilised in emergency situations, especially where there is the prospect of a family being split up and children taken into care. This is in addition to the powers of the social services department to provide temporary emergency accommodation (see below, pp. 10–13).

2. Rehousing

The duty to rehouse is owed to those who are displaced from their home by local authority or other public activity, and requires the local authority to provide suitable alternative residential accommodation on reasonable terms, if it is not otherwise available to the displaced person.

a. When the duty to rehouse arises

The circumstances in which a duty to rehouse will arise are outlined in s.39 of the Land Compensation Act 1973, as amended by Schedule 13, para 40, of the Housing Act 1974. The Act envisages four situations: where a person is displaced from residential accommodation on any land in consequence of:

(*a*) the acquisition of the land by an authority possessing (but not necessarily exercising) compulsory purchase powers;

(*b*) the making of a housing order, or the acceptance of an undertaking, in respect of a house or building on the land;

(*c*) where the land has already been acquired by an authority possessing compulsory purchase powers or appropriated by a local authority and is being held for the time being by the authority for the purposes for which it was acquired or appropriated, the carrying out of any improvement to a house or building on the land or of any redevelopment on the land;

(*d*) the service of an improvement notice under Part VIII of the Housing Act 1974.

i. *Displacement as the immediate result of acquisition or appropriation by an authority with powers of compulsory purchase*

Detailed consideration of the circumstances in which compulsory purchase powers can be exercised by a council or other public authority (e.g. a statutory undertaker such as an electricity board) is beyond the scope of this book. See generally J. K. Boynton, *Compulsory Purchase and Compensation*, Oyez Practice Notes No. 53, 3rd Edn (Oyez Publishing Limited).

Whenever such powers are exercised, however, a residential occupier who is displaced as a result must be rehoused by the *local* authority (i.e. not necessarily by the *displacing* authority). Furthermore, it is clear from the wording of s.39(1)(*a*) that the duty to rehouse also arises if a person is displaced from land which was acquired voluntarily, i.e. by agreement with its owner, if the relevant authority had power to acquire that land by compulsory purchase instead of, or in default of, agreement.

For example, a local authority may purchase, by agreement or compulsorily, a house which is unfit for human habitation and incapable of repair at a reasonable expense (see pp. 36–37). If such a house is acquired by agreement and the occupants displaced, a duty to rehouse will arise; s.39(1)(*a*) requires only that the acquiring authority *possess* compulsory purchase powers, not that such powers are in fact exercised.

Local authorities have compulsory purchase powers under Parts II and III of the Housing Act 1957, which accompany their powers to make demolition, closing, or clearance orders. Part II is directed to the compulsory improvement of individual dwellings, and is considered more fully in the next chapter.

ii. *Displacement as the result of a housing order made, or an undertaking accepted, by a local authority.*

A housing order can take any one of three forms: a demolition order, a closing order, or a clearance order.

A demolition order is a direction that specified premises be demolished within a given time by the person to whom the direction is given (ss.19–26 H.A. 1957).

A closing order is a direction prohibiting the use of specified premises for any purpose other than one approved by the local authority (s.27 H.A. 1957), and can be made against part only of a building (s.18(1)(*a*) H.A. 1957).

A clearance order is an order for the demolition, by the recipient of the order, of designated premises within a clearance area. A clearance area is a particular district consisting largely of unfit, dangerous, or unhealthy housing which the local authority considers can best be dealt with by wholesale demolition. Before declaring a clearance area the local authority must be satisfied that suitable alternative accommodation will be available for displaced persons as and when needed; if such accommodation will not otherwise be available, the loca authority must itself be able to provide it (s.42(1) H.A. 1957). No further clearance orders under Part III of the Housing Act 1957 can be made after 31st August 1974, and those made before that date cannot be implemented after 1st September 1975 (s.108 H.A. 1974).

Under Part II of the Housing Act 1957 a local authority can order the demolition or closing of any house which is unfit for human habitation and cannot be made fit at a reasonable expense (s.17(1) H.A. 1957). Under s.60 of the Housing Act 1969, a closing order can be made against part of a house in multiple occupation, if that house is not, and cannot at a reasonable expense be, provided with the necessary means of escape from fire, but such means of escape would or could be adequately provided if part of the house were not used for human habitation.

As an alternative to closing or demolition in a Part II case, the local authority may accept an undertaking from any owner or mortgagee of the premises, either to make them reasonably fit for human habitation, or not to use them for that purpose (s.16(4) H.A. 1957). If the undertaking is dishonoured, either by failure to carry out the necessary works in time or by using the premises in violation of the terms of the undertaking, the authority must proceed to make a demolition or closing order, or to purchase the premises (ss. 17(1) and 17(2) H.A. 1957). An undertaking can also be accepted under s.60 of the 1969 Act that the designated part of a house in multiple occupation will not be used for human habitation.

Finally, undertakings can be accepted under s.87 of the Housing Act 1974 that premises to which the undertaking relates will be improved in specified respects (see p. 42).

A person who gives an undertaking or against whom a housing order is made can recover possession of the designated premises in the County court, the Rent Act 1968 notwithstanding. A protected, statutory or Part VI tenant thus loses his security of tenure (ss. 16(5), 22(5), 27(5) H.A. 1957, s.60(7) H.A. 1969).

Possession can be recovered by the landlord even though the condition of the premises which has led to the order was brought about by the landlord's own breach of contractual or statutory duty (*Buswell* v. *Goodwin* [1971] 1 W.L.R. 92 (C.A.)).

iii. *Displacement as the result of improvement or redevelopment by a local authority of land previously acquired*

This heading covers the situation in which displacement is not an immediate consequence of acquisition or appropriation by the authority, but of eventual improvement (including alteration or enlargement) or redevelopment (including a change of use). For example, single dwellings or blocks of houses may be acquired by a local authority as part of a long-term programme of redevelopment or renewal. As and when that programme is implemented, displaced residents must be rehoused.

As under i. above, the land or building may have been

acquired compulsorily or by agreement. A duty to rehouse will exist whenever the authority had power to acquire the land by compulsory purchase even if that power was not exercised.

iv. *Displacement as the result of an improvement notice served under Part VIII of the Housing Act 1974*

A person on whom an improvement notice has been served has the right, when the notice comes into effect, to take any reasonable steps against an occupying tenant to implement the terms of the notice (s.96(2) H.A. 1974). This may involve the temporary, indefinite, or permanent displacement of the tenant. If the displacement is not permanent the tenant has no right to be rehoused (s.39(6A) L.C.A. 1973), but an improvement notice will not be served in the first place unless the local authority is satisfied that proper short and long term housing arrangements have been made for the tenant. These must be agreed in writing by the tenant on the one side and the landlord or local authority on the other (s.86 H.A. 1974). An order can be made, however, if the tenant unreasonably refuses to accede to these arrangements (s. 88(2)(*d*) H.A. 1974).

b. Qualification for rehousing

i. *When the land is acquired by compulsory purchase*

A person is not regarded as having been displaced so as to qualify to be rehoused unless he was residing (i.e. made a home) in the premises at the time when notice of making a compulsory purchase order was first published and prior to its submission for confirmation to the central government; or, if confirmation is not required, at the time when notice of preparation of the order in draft was first published (s.39(6)(*a*) L.C.A. 1973).

ii. *When the land is acquired by agreement by an authority possessing compulsory purchase powers*

In this case, a person qualifies only if he was residing in the relevant premises at the time when the agreement was made (s.39(6)(*c*) L.C.A. 1973).

iii. *When the land is acquired under an Act of Parliament which specifies the land as subject to compulsory purchase*

Here a person qualifies for rehousing only if he was residing in the relevant premises when the provisions of the Bill were first published (s.39(6)(*b*) L.C.A. 1973).

iv. *When displacement is in consequence of a housing order made, improvement notice served, or undertaking accepted, by a local authority*

In order to qualify to be rehoused, a person must have been residing in the relevant accommodation at the time when the order was made, the notice served, or the undertaking accepted.

However, certain persons are *not* entitled to be rehoused despite satisfying the above requirements. These are:

(*a*) trespassers, and those who have been permitted to reside in any house or building on the land pending its demolition or improvement;

(*b*) those who were owner-occupiers of the premises from which they have been displaced, and who have been advanced money by the local authority, under s.41 of the Land Compensation Act 1973, in order to acquire or construct another dwelling;

(*c*) those who have been advanced money by the local authority under the Small Dwellings Acquisition Acts 1899–1923, or under s.43 of the Housing (Financial Provisions) Act 1958, or by a development corporation or the Commission for New Towns, in order to acquire alternative accommodation; and (*d*) those who caused the land to be acquired in the first place by serving a blight notice under s.192 of the Town and Country Planning Act 1971.

c. 'Suitable alternative accommodation on reasonable terms'

What must a local authority do in order to discharge its duty to rehouse and what sanctions are available to the aggrieved individual against the local authority, if this duty is not discharged? These questions were considered by the Court of Appeal in *R.* v. *Bristol Corporation, ex parte Hendy* [1974] 1 W.L.R. 498, on an application for an order of *mandamus*.

A closing order had been made against the flat of which the applicant was protected tenant; as a result the landlord obtained an order for possession from the County court and the tenant was evicted. The local authority lodged him and his family in temporary accommodation, promising them a regular council tenancy as soon as a suitable dwelling became available. The displaced tenant contended that this was not 'suitable alternative accommodation on reasonable terms', to which he was entitled under s.39, and he applied for an order of *mandamus* to compel the local authority to fulfil its duty.

The Court of Appeal decided that a displaced person is not entitled to absolute priority over those on the housing waiting list. Displacement is simply a factor to be taken into account by the local authority when housing stock is allocated. The duty under s.39 of the Land Compensation Act 1973 is therefore fulfilled by providing *temporary* accommodation which is suitable to the present needs of the displaced person or family, if this is the best that can be done at the time, so long as the authority thereafter acts reasonably in providing a tenancy with equivalent security of tenure to that previously enjoyed, as soon as practicable. A council tenancy on usual council terms is sufficient in this respect.

d. Enforcement

There is no provision for enforcing the duty under s.39. An aggrieved person must therefore seek an order of *mandamus*, the granting of which lies in the discretion of a divisional court of the Queen's Bench Division of the High Court. In *Hendy's* case, *mandamus* would not have been granted even if, on the given facts, the local authority *had* been in breach of duty under s.39, since the authority had done the best it could for the time being, and was prepared to provide permanent accommodation as soon as practicable.

3. Emergency accommodation

a. Government policy

In D.H.S.S. Circular No. 18/74 of 7th February 1974 the policy of the central government towards homelessness is clearly delineated. It is seen to be the responsibility of local authorities to deal with the homelessness of individuals and families in their areas, wherever those in need came from and however the homelessness arose. People should not be turned away simply because they originated from the district of another local authority, or even if their homelessness could be attributed to their own fault.

This responsibility is seen to be a joint charge upon the housing and social services departments, although it is regarded principally as the function of the housing department to provide the requisite accommodation. Social services departments should fulfil a complementary function of giving advice and assistance, in order to anticipate and forestall homelessness, or to ensure, so far as possible, that it does not recur. This might include the giving of advice on tenants' rights, to lessen the incidence of homelessness through unlawful eviction, or matrimonial guidance and counselling to reduce homelessness caused by family disputes.

The philosophy expressed in the circular is summed up in paragraph 8: 'The Government believes that all those who have no roof, or appear likely to lose their shelter within a month, should be helped to secure accommodation by advice, preventive action, or, if these are not enough, the provision, permanently or temporarily, of local authority accommodation'.

b. The law

i. *The duty to provide necessary accommodation*

Unfortunately, the attitude and policy of the central government is not the law, unless expressed in legislation. The *legal* entitlement of an individual or family to accommodation, even of a temporary sort in emergency situations, is closely circumscribed. The governing statutory provision is s.21(1) (*b*) of the National Assistance Act 1948, as amended by Schedule 23 of the Local Government Act 1972. The amended section came into force on 1st April 1974 and provides that:

> a local authority may with the approval of the Secretary of State, and to such extent as he may direct shall, make arrangements for providing . . . temporary accommodation for persons who are in urgent need thereof, being need arising in circumstances which could not reasonably have been foreseen or in such other circumstances as the authority may in any particular case determine.

In its unamended form, s.21(1)(*b*) imposed a *duty* upon local authorities to provide temporary accommodation in cases of urgency. Although the 1972 Act substitutes a *power* for this duty, so that local authorities remain able, but are no longer *obliged* to provide emergency shelter, it is generally believed that the original obligatory status of s.21(1)(*b*) has now been restored, as the result of a ministerial directive: D/N120/8 of 11th February 1974.

ii. *Administration*

Responsibility under s.21(1)(*b*) is placed upon the social services department of a local authority by s.7(1) of the Local

Authority Social Services Act 1970. Since the reorganisation of local government, social services fall to the *county* council of a non-metropolitan county, and the *district* council of a metropolitan county, whereas housing is a function of district councils throughout the country. This distribution of functions appears to have caused a degree of uncertainty and confusion in some areas, which has been aggravated still further by the policy expressed in Circular 18/74 (above, p. 10) of eventually transferring all housing matters to housing departments and away from social services departments. The restored *duty* to provide emergency accommodation is seen by the central government as a holding measure until this transition is complete.

iii. '*Urgent and unforseeable need*'

It will be noticed that the duty to provide temporary accommodation is confined to situations of urgent and unforeseeable need. In other words, s.21(1)(*b*) aims to alleviate acute rather than chronic housing problems, and, moreover, only those which the victim could not reasonably anticipate or forestall. The section therefore applies to homelessness arising from a natural disaster such as fire or flood, or from a sudden crime such as forcible entry or unlawful eviction, but not to homelessness arising from a foreseeable event such as lawful eviction for failure to pay the rent.

iv. *Enforcement*

No sanction is laid down in the National Assistance Act 1948 or the Local Government Act 1972 for enforcing the obligation under s.21(1)(*b*). However, under s.25(1) of the 1948 Act, the Supplementary Benefits Commission can require a local authority to provide accommodation, if the Commission is satisfied that a person in the area of that local authority is in urgent need. Otherwise an aggrieved person would be obliged to apply for an order of *mandamus* to compel the local authority to perform its statutory duty. The granting of such an order, as we have seen, lies in the discretion of a divisional court of the Queen's Bench Division.

v. *Other provisions*

In addition to the duty under s.21(1)(*b*), a local authority has the *power* to provide temporary accommodation in whatever circumstances are deemed appropriate. This may be done either in premises managed by the local authority itself, by another local authority, or by a voluntary organisation such as the Salvation Army (s.26 N.A.A. 1948).

The local authority must also provide *residential* accommodation for those in need of care and attention, such as the old or infirm, if such accommodation is not available elsewhere (s.21(1)(*a*) N.A.A. 1948).

CHAPTER 2

REPAIR AND MAINTENANCE OF RENTED ACCOMMODATION

1. Generally

The responsibilities of a landlord and his tenant for the state of the premises at the onset of the tenancy, and for their maintenance and repair thereafter, are to be found partly in statute and partly in common law. The scope of these responsibilities may differ according to the nature of the tenancy or the type of premises.

Generally speaking, those obligations which are implied into a landlord and tenant relationship by the *common law* can be restricted or excluded by the express agreement of the parties, and an express undertaking of a more limited nature than that which would otherwise be implied overrides the common law: *expressum facit cessare tacitum*. On the other hand, obligations which are deemed to be incorporated into a tenancy by *statute* cannot, generally speaking, be excluded or restricted.

In strict terminology a *covenant* is a term in a deed under seal. Therefore, if there is no lease, in the sense of a deed under seal, there can be no covenants, but only contractual terms (i.e. conditions and warranties) in an agreement for a lease. Some statutory provisions, e.g. s.32 of the Housing Act 1961, purport to imply *covenants*; others, such as s.6 of the Housing Act 1957, to imply *conditions* or *undertakings*. However, too strict a view should not be taken of this terminological divergence: since the word 'covenant' is now generally used to describe a term in a lease or an agreement for a lease, one may assume, in the absence of clear indications to the contrary, that provisions such as s.32 of the Housing Act 1961 apply in any landlord and tenant relationship.

2. The landlord's implied liabilities

a. Furnished tenancies: implied condition of fitness

There is a condition implied by the common law into lettings of furnished dwellings that the premises will be reasonably fit for human habitation at the commencement of the tenancy (but not thereafter: *Sarson* v. *Roberts* [1895] 2 Q.B. 395 (C.A.))

i. *Standard of fitness*

There is no predetermined standard of fitness here (cf. s.4 of the Housing Act 1957); each case turns on its own particular circumstances. Premises have been held to be unfit, so as to break the implied condition, when:

(*a*) they were infested with insects (*Smith* v. *Marrable* (1843) 11 M. & W. 5);

(*b*) the drainage system was seriously defective (*Wilson* v. *Finch Hatton* (1877) 2 Ex.D. 336);

(*c*) a recent occupant had been suffering from an infectious disease leaving 'an actual and appreciable risk to the tenant, his family, or household' (*Collins* v. *Hopkins* [1923] 2 K.B. 617).

ii. *Strict duty*

The duty cast upon the landlord is a strict one; it is not discharged by taking reasonable care to ensure the fitness of the premises or by entertaining an honest belief that the premises are fit. The landlord is liable if the premises are not in fact fit.

iii. *The meaning of 'furnished'*

This is an area where the otherwise largely defunct distinction between a furnished and an unfurnished tenancy remains relevant. It by no means follows, however, that the tests and standards employed, prior to the Rent Act 1974, to determine whether a tenancy was unprotected by virtue of being furnished apply here. Since the general policy is to extend the protection of the Rent Acts and of this implied condition (see *Collins* v. *Hopkins* above), there is ample reason to suppose that the Rent Act criteria should not be utilised. For example, one may assume that a fully furnished dwelling, as in *Woodward* v. *Docherty* [1974] 1 W.L.R. 966 (C.A.), would attract the implied condition of fitness, although the dwelling in that case was held not to be furnished for the purposes of s.2 of the Rent Act 1968. Furthermore, under s.2 a substantial part of the rent must have been fairly attributable to furniture, fairness being determined according to the value of the furniture to the tenant. No such requirement need be fulfilled in order to imply the condition of fitness for human habitation.

iv. *Exclusion of implied condition*

The implied condition can be excluded or qualified by agreement between the parties. It would be curtailed, for example, by the presence in the tenancy agreement of an *express* obligation of fitness, albeit of more limited scope.

b. Unfurnished tenancies

There is no covenant or condition implied by the common law that a dwelling which is let unfurnished shall be fit for human habitation or for any other purpose, or that the landlord will repair or maintain the rented premises.

c. Tenancies of a 'small house'

i. *Implied liabilities*

Section 6 of the Housing Act 1957 implies into a contract for the letting of a so-called small house a 'condition' that the dwelling is fit for human habitation at the beginning of the tenancy, and an 'undertaking' that it will be kept fit by the landlord during the tenancy. The parties cannot contract out of, or limit, this double liability. The obligations are implied whether the tenancy is furnished or unfurnished.

The condition and undertaking apply to any dwelling (including part of a house, even a single room) which satisfies the test of a 'small house' and which is let for human habitation, but they do not apply if the tenancy is for at least three years; is not determinable by either party within that time, and the lessee has covenanted to make the premises fit for human habitation.

Apparently the condition is not to be implied if the dwelling is incapable of being made fit at a reasonable expense (*Buswell* v. *Goodwin* [1971] 1 W.L.R. 92 (C.A.)), although it is not clear whether the reasoning of this case extends to the *undertaking* also. On the other hand, a house may be unfit for human habitation even though the particular defect can be remedied quickly and at little expense (*per* LORD ATKIN in *Summers* v. *Salford Corporation* [1943] A.C. 283 at 288 (H.L.)).

ii. *The meaning of 'small house'*

A 'small house' is defined by reference to the gross annual rent payable under the tenancy agreement and not, as might be expected, the dimensions of the rented premises. If the contract of letting was made before 31st July 1923, the agreed rent for the premises must not exceed £40 per annum within the then administrative county of London, or £26 per annum in a borough or urban district with a population at the last census of 50,000 or more or £16 per annum elsewhere.

If the contract was made between 31st July 1923 and 5th July 1957, the agreed rent must not exceed £40 per annum in the then administrative county of London or £26 elsewhere.

If the contract was made between 6th July 1957 and 31st March 1965, the agreed rent must not exceed £80 per annum in the then administrative county of London or £52 per annum elsewhere.

And finally, if the contract was made on or after 1st April

1965, the agreed rent must not exceed £80 in the City of London, the Temples, or an inner London borough or £52 elsewhere.

iii. *Requirement of Notice*

The landlord is not liable under the implied undertaking unless and until he has received notice that the premises are unfit, but it is an open question whether the landlord will become liable if he learns of the defects from a source other than the tenant (*Morgan* v. *Liverpool Corporation* [1927] 2 K.B. 131 (C.A.)). Hence a landlord will not be answerable for injury caused to the tenant by a defect of which the landlord was unaware, but he will become liable to repair that defect once he learns of it (*O'Brien* v. *Robinson* [1973] A.C. 912 (H.L.)).

The landlord, or an agent with his written authorisation, is entitled to inspect the condition of the premises at any reasonable time of the day, on giving the tenant twenty-four hours' notice in writing.

iv. *Standard of fitness*

The standard of fitness at which premises are to be maintained for the purposes of these implied obligations is set out in s.4 of the Housing Act 1957. A house is unfit for human habitation if, and only if, it is so defective in respect of one or more listed particulars as not to be reasonably suitable for occupation. The list of particulars is as follows:

(*a*) Repair;
(*b*) Stability;
(*c*) Freedom from damp;
[(*cc*) Internal arrangement;]
(*d*) Natural lighting;
(*e*) Ventilation;
(*f*) Water supply;
(*g*) Drainage and sanitary conveniences;

(*h*) Facilities for . . . preparation and cooking of food and for the disposal of waste water.

'Internal arrangement' (i.e. the layout of rooms and amenities) was added to the list, and 'facilities for the storage of food' removed, by s.71 of the Housing Act 1969. Under s.32 of the Public Health Act 1961, a local authority can now compel the owner of a house, or any building which is occupied as a separate dwelling, to provide sufficient and suitable accommodation for the storage of food.

It will be noticed that the list above does not include such items as internal decorative repair, freedom from vermin or other infestation (but see *Stanton* v. *Southwick* [1920] 2 K.B. 642 (D.C.)), freedom from risk of disease, adequate heating, suitable fire precautions or escapes, or the provision of all the basic amenities. A dwelling is therefore to be regarded as fit for human habitation even if seriously defective in respect of matters which are not itemised in s.4.

Whether or not a defect, or a cumulation of defects, is sufficient to render a dwelling unfit for human habitation depends upon the circumstances of each individual case. With regard to the state of repair of the premises, ATKIN L.J. suggested that a dwelling is not reasonably fit for human habitation if, as a consequence of the state of repair, injury (whether to life, limb, or health) may be suffered in the ordinary course of using the premises (*Morgan* v. *Liverpool Corporation*, above, p. 18).

In order for premises to be unfit for human habitation, it is not necessary that they be in a general state of disrepair. Specific and single items of disrepair, such as a jammed window, can, in appropriate circumstances, suffice (*Summers* v. *Salford Corporation*, above, p. 17).

'Repair' comprehends not only the structural condition of the premises, but such other matters as electrical wiring and landlord's fixtures, e.g. a curtain rail. It does not extend to defects in any furniture supplied under the tenancy, as this does not relate to the condition of the *house*, but to things *in* the house.

v. *Remedies*

Breach of this implied undertaking can lead to damages being recovered for personal injury to the tenant, for the cost of replacing or repairing the tenant's furniture, for the cost of decorative work done by the tenant, and for inconvenience and discomfort (*Walker* v. *Hobbs & Co.* (1889) 23 Q.B.D. 458 (D.C.), *Horrex* v. *Pidwell* [1958] C.L.Y. 1461 (Cty. ct.)).

The tenant is also entitled to give up the tenancy.

d. Short tenancies

i. *The implied undertaking*

By s.32 of the Housing Act 1961 a covenant is implied into a short lease of a dwelling-house (and, presumably, a condition into an agreement for a short lease) that the landlord will keep the structure and exterior of the dwelling-house in repair, and keep the installations for the supply of water, gas and electricity, and for space heating and water heating, in repair and proper working order.

This obligation cannot be excluded or limited except by an order of the County court made with the consent of the parties, and any covenant or condition in the lease or agreement which obliges the tenant to repair or maintain the premises is ineffective insofar as it impinges upon the areas covered by the implied undertaking.

The tenant is nevertheless still bound to use the premises in a tenant-like manner (see below, pp. 27–8) and he *can* validly undertake to rebuild or reinstate the premises in case of destruction or damage by fire, flood, or inevitable accident, and to keep in repair anything which the tenant is entitled to remove from the premises. Even if the tenant does not make any agreement in respect of these matters, the landlord is not liable for them under the implied covenant or condition.

ii. *The meaning of 'short tenancy'*

The undertaking is implied into a so-called short tenancy, i.e. one for a term of less than seven years, including a periodic tenancy. A tenancy which, though granted for seven years or more, is determinable within seven years at the unfettered discretion of the landlord, is to be regarded as a short tenancy for the purposes of s.32. It is not sufficient, however, that the landlord has an option to terminate which is dependent upon a contingency that might or might not occur within seven years, e.g. an option arising upon someone's death, or upon a breach of covenant by the tenant (s.33(1) and (2), *Parker* v. *O'Connor* [1974] 1 W.L.R. 1160 (C.A.)).

iii. *The scope of the obligation*

The obligation is in two parts, the first relating to the structure and exterior of the dwelling, the second to certain installations within the dwelling:

'*Structure and exterior*' are not defined in the Act, although drains, gutters, and external pipes are specifically included. Certainly the maintenance of the structure does not comprehend matters of mere decorative repair, but beyond this it is not clear what defects should be classified as non-structural. For example, is internal plasterwork a structural matter? Are stair-rods holding a carpet, or even internal doors, part of the structure? It has been decided that windows *are* part of the structure of a house (*Boswell* v. *Crucible Steel Co.* [1925] 1 K.B. 119 (C.A.), which suggests that the standard obligation placed upon local authority tenants to replace broken windows is invalid, at least where the breakage is not caused by the tenant's default. (Where it is caused by the tenant's default it will constitute a breach of the tenant's obligation not to commit voluntary waste, or the obligation to use the premises in a tenant-like manner, see below, p. 27.) As to possible meanings of the word 'structure', see Woodfall, *Landlord and Tenant*, 27th Edn, Vol. 1, para. 1486.

The exterior of a dwelling can include steps and a pathway, if they form a necessary access to the dwelling. Generally speaking, yards, gardens, fences and outhouses are not part of the exterior of the dwelling for the purposes of s.32 (*Brown* v. *Liverpool Corporation* [1969] 3 All E.R. 1345 (C.A.) cf.

Hopwood v. *Cannock Chase District Council* [1975] 1 All E.R. 796 (C.A.)). In *Brown*'s case the fact that the defective pathway was very short was influential in persuading the court that it was part of the exterior and so within s.32.

The onus of proof is upon the tenant to establish a breach of the implied undertaking (*Foster* v. *Day* (1968) 208 E.G. 495 (C.A.)).

The *installations* which must be kept in repair and proper working order include basins, sinks, baths and sanitary conveniences, but exclude any fixture, fitting, or appliance for making use of the water, gas, or electricity supply. Hence the landlord is not liable to replace defective lightbulbs, for example. However, the landlord is also responsible under s.32 for the maintenance of space heating and water heating installations: he would therefore be liable to replace a broken gas or electric fire, provided that the tenant were not to blame for its state, and provided that the tenant is not the owner or otherwise entitled to remove it from the dwelling.

The three implied covenants, conditions, or undertakings considered above all carry forward into a statutory tenancy, by virtue of s.12(1) of the Rent Act 1968. They give rise to contractual obligations and so can be enforced by the tenant alone. It is likely that the landlord is not in breach of these obligations until he has been informed of the need for repair (*McCarrick* v. *Liverpool Corporation* [1947] A.C. 219 (H.L.)).

3. The landlord's statutory liability under the Defective Premises Act 1972

a. The duty of care

Section 4 of the Defective Premises Act 1972 imposes upon a landlord a duty of care which is owed to all persons, including the tenant, who might reasonably be expected to be put at risk by certain defects in the state of the rented premises. This duty, which replaces that formerly owed under s.4 of the Occupiers' Liability Act 1957, is to take such care as is reasonable in all the circumstances to see that those to whom the duty is owed are reasonably safe from personal injury or from damage to their property caused by a so-called 'relevant defect'.

b. The meaning of 'relevant defect'

A 'relevant defect' is a defect in the state of the premises which satisfies the following requirements:

(*a*) it exists on or after 1st January 1974 (the commencement date of the Act) if the tenancy began before that date. Provided the tenancy began after 31st December 1973, however, it is sufficient that the defect exists on or after the earliest of the following three times: the time when the tenancy begins, the time when the tenancy agreement is made, or the time when possession is taken of the premises in contemplation of a letting.

(*b*) the defect must arise from, or continue because of, an act or omission of the landlord, and that act or omission must be a breach of an obligation owed to the tenant to repair or maintain the premises, or would be such a breach if the landlord had been given notice of the defect. The source of the obligation owed to the tenant can be contractual or statutory.

Furthermore, if the tenancy, either expressly or by implication, gives the landlord a *right* to enter premises in order to carry out any maintenance or repair, such a right is to be treated as an *obligation* of an equivalent extent for the purposes of s.4. This notional obligation is deemed to arise from the time that the landlord first is, or can put himself, in a position to exercise the right to enter. The landlord is not, however, to be regarded as under an obligation in respect of defects which arise from or continue because of a breach by the tenant of any *express* obligation in the tenancy. (As to a tenant's *implied* obligations, see below, pp. 26–9.)

c. When the duty arises

The duty imposed by s.4 will therefore arise where the landlord is under an express or implied repairing obligation, e.g. by virtue of s.32 of the Housing Act 1961, and where the landlord has an express or implied right to enter and repair or maintain, provided that the need for repair or maintenance is not brought about by the tenant's breach of an express obligation. The landlord's duty relates only to those defects which it is his right or duty under the tenancy to repair.

In *Mint* v. *Good* [1951] 1 K.B. 517 (C.A.) SOMERVELL L.J. expressed the opinion that it is not difficult to imply into a contract for a *weekly* tenancy a right on the landlord's part to enter and do necessary repairs. This would suffice to give rise to the duty of care under s.4, unless the tenant owes an express duty to repair or maintain in respect of the same defects.

The landlord's duty of care will only arise if he knows, or ought in all the circumstances to have known, of the relevant defect.

d. Extent of the duty

The provisions of s.4 of the Defective Premises Act 1972 apply not only to defects in premises occupied under a tenancy, but to defects in premises occupied under any other contract or under a statutory provision. The Act thus applies to contractual licences and statutory tenancies (see below, pp. 96–106 and 117–120) also.

The landlord cannot contract out of, or limit, the liability imposed by s.4; any term of an agreement which, directly or indirectly, purports to exclude or restrict that liability is void (s.6(3) D.P.A. 1972).

4. THE LANDLORD'S LIABILITY FOR THE CONDITION OF PARTS RETAINED BY HIM

a. Common law

A landlord who lets a part of his premises and retains

occupation or control of the remainder owes the tenant a common law duty to take reasonable care that the retained premises are not in such a state as to injure the tenant or diminish his enjoyment of the premises which have been let to him (*Cockburn* v. *Smith* [1924] 2 K.B. 119 (C.A.) where the Court of Appeal left undecided the question whether this duty arises in contract or in tort, cf. *Miller* v. *Hancock* [1893] 2 Q.B. 177 (C.A.)).

The duty applies not only to another dwelling retained by the landlord but to such parts of the premises as a common roof, staircase, garden or path. It is not necessarily cut down by an express undertaking of more limited scope. For example, an express agreement by the landlord to repair or maintain a common staircase would not exclude his liability in respect of a common roof. The test appears to be whether or not the interest of the tenant in the part covered by the express undertaking is the same as his interest in the part in respect of which the tenant claims the protection of the implied duty. If it is the same, for example where the tenant has been given a licence to use the landlord's stairs and corridors, an express undertaking to maintain the one will exclude the implied duty in respect of the other, on the principle *expressum facit cessare tacitum*. On the other hand, the implied duty would not be excluded in respect of parts retained by the landlord over which the tenant had been given no licence, for example a common roof (*Cockburn* v. *Smith*, above).

b. The Occupiers' Liability Act 1957

Section 4 of the Defective Premises Act 1972 applies only to defects in the rented premises (see above, p. 22). However, if the landlord retains control of other premises, e.g. paths, stairways or corridors, which the tenant, his household, and his visitors must use in order to gain access to the rented dwelling, the landlord is placed under the 'common duty of care' towards those people with regard to the state of the premises over which he has retained control. This duty, imposed by s.2 of the Occupiers' Liability Act 1957, is to take such care as is reasonable in all the circumstances to see that the tenant, his household, and his visitors will be reasonably safe, when using the landlord's premises for permitted purposes.

So far as the tenant is concerned, this statutory provision adds little to the protection already afforded him by the common law, except that the Occupiers' Liability Act clearly imposes a duty in tort. The common law did not extend the same degree of protection to all others, however (*Indermaur* v. *Dames* (1866) L.R. 1 C.P. 274 at 288 *per* WILLES J.). The Occupiers' Liability Act imposes the same duty of care towards all lawful visitors to the landlord's premises.

The duty owed to the tenant can be restricted or excluded; the duty owed to third parties cannot (s.3 O.L.A. 1957).

5. THE TENANT'S IMPLIED LIABILITIES

It is very common to find, in a lease or written agreement for a lease, a term which places responsibility upon the tenant to repair, maintain or decorate the rented premises to some extent. Such a term is valid only in so far as it does not impinge upon the landlord's unavoidable statutory obligations (e.g. those imposed by s.32 H.A. 1961, but note also s.147 of the Law of Property Act 1925, under which a court has power to relieve a tenant from an obligation to maintain the premises in good decorative order).

a. Weekly tenancies

In the absence of an express undertaking, however, a tenant's liability is limited. A *weekly* tenant is liable in two respects only: he must not commit so-called voluntary waste, and he must use the premises in the manner of a good tenant. This second aspect of his liability in fact comprehends the first.

i. *Voluntary waste*

Voluntary waste is positive action by the tenant, or those for whom he is responsible, which damages the premises or alters their nature or character. Whether or not the nature or character of premises has been altered is a question of fact; (*Hyman* v. *Rose* [1912] A.C. 623 (H.L.): the change must be in the premises, not just in the use to which they are put).

The act may be deliberate or negligent, e.g. carelessly smashing a window is voluntary waste. Voluntary waste may, in fact, even *improve* the dwelling or its value, in which case it is known as ameliorating waste.

A tenant is liable for voluntary waste. This liability may be based upon an implied contractual obligation, or it may stem from a common law duty apart from the contract (see *Marsden* v. *Edward Heyes Ltd* [1927] 2 K.B. 1 (C.A.) cf. *per* LORD DENNING in *Regis Property Co. Ltd* v. *Dudley* [1959] A.C. 370 at 407 (H.L.)).

Case 3 of Schedule 3, Part 1 of the Rent Act 1968 enables a court in its discretion to make an order restoring possession to the landlord, where the condition of the dwelling-house has, in the opinion of the court, deteriorated owing to acts of waste by the tenant, anyone residing or lodging with him, or any sub-tenant. If the acts of waste are those of a lodger or sub-tenant, however, possession will not be restored to the landlord unless the tenant has failed to take such steps as were reasonably available to him to remove the culprit.

ii. *Tenant-like user*

Liability for voluntary waste signifies an obligation not to commit deleterious acts, but, apart from any express undertaking, a weekly tenant is not obliged to *keep* the rented premises in repair; he need not act positively to prevent the premises from deteriorating of their own accord.

Nevertheless the tenant must use the premises in a manner which befits a good tenant. In addition to avoiding acts of voluntary waste he must do such small and inexpensive jobs of maintenance and repair as it is reasonable to expect from a good tenant, such as mending fuses, unblocking the sink, sweeping chimneys, cleaning the windows, and turning off mains supplies when leaving the premises for any length of time. Beyond this the tenant is not liable: deterioration in the state of the premises is not, in the absence of an express undertaking, his responsibility (*Warren* v. *Keen* [1954] 1 Q.B. 15).

b. Other periodic tenancies

The precise extent of liability under a non-weekly tenancy is unclear. While it is certainly not *less* than that of a weekly tenant, it may well be no greater. Oddly enough, this question has yet to be resolved by the courts or by the legislature (see the observations of the Court of Appeal in *Warren* v. *Keen*, above). It has been said that a tenant for years, such as a fixed term tenant (Law of Property Act 1925 s.206(xxvii) below, p. 113), is liable for *permissive* waste, that is, for allowing the premises to deteriorate through failure to maintain or repair (*per* PARKE B. in *Yellowly* v. *Gower* (1855) 11 Ex. 274 at 293, 4); but against this stand the assertions of LORD DENNING in both *Warren* v. *Keen*, above, (where the tenancy in question was weekly) and *Regis Property Co. Ltd* v. *Dudley*, above, p. 27, (which concerned a monthly tenancy) that the liability of a tenant for *any* term does not extend beyond express obligation, voluntary waste, and tenant-like user.

It has also been said that a *yearly* tenant must keep the premises wind- and water-tight, but it is doubtful whether this vague phrase adds anything to the obligation of tenant-like user.

Under Case 3 of Schedule 3, Part 1 of the Rent Act 1968 (above, p. 27), possession can be recovered if the condition of the rented dwelling has deteriorated not only as a result of acts of waste but also through the neglect or default of the tenant, anyone residing or lodging with him, or a sub-tenant. The scope of the phrase 'neglect or default' is not suggested in the

Act, but presumably it must be confined to a breach by the tenant of the obligations considered above. Case 3 repeats a ground of possession which was available under earlier legislation (The Rent and Mortgage Interest Restrictions (Amendment) Act 1933, Schedule 1 para. (*b*)) and no point was taken in *Warren* v. *Keen* that it imposes any liability for permissive waste.

6. Specific enforcement of repairing obligations

Until quite recently it was generally believed that the specific performance of a repairing obligation, whether the liability fell upon the landlord or the tenant, would not be ordered. Authority for this proposition was apparently to be found in the judgment of Lord Eldon in *Hill* v. *Barclay* (1810) 16 Ves. 402, a case dealing with the equitable jurisdiction to grant relief against forfeiture. Lord Eldon suggested lack of mutuality as the reason why specific performance would not be ordered.

More recently, Lord Wilberforce stated that specific performance of repairing covenants cannot be granted because the court is unable to supervise the work, but he acknowledged that relief against forfeiture for non-compliance with a repairing obligation can be given if the work has eventually been done and relief would be equitable in all the circumstances (*Shiloh Spinners* v. *Harding* [1973] A.C. 691; n.b. also s.146 L.P.A. 1925; s.31 R.A. 1965; and s.10(1) R.A. 1968).

However, in *Jeune* v. *Queen's Cross Properties Ltd* [1973] 3 W.L.R. 378 Pennycuick, v-c ruled that specific performance of a *landlord's* repairing covenant can be ordered in certain circumstances. A comparison was drawn with the circumstances in which specific performance of a building contract may be ordered. Three conditions need to be satisfied: first, damages must not be an adequate remedy; second, the work to be done must be sufficiently clear; and, third, the defendant must be in possession of the premises so that the plaintiff cannot do the work himself without committing a trespass. In *Jeune's* case, the premises in question had been retained by the landlord.

PENNYCUICK V-C accepted *Hill* v. *Barclay* as authority for the proposition that a *tenant's* covenant to repair cannot be specifically enforced.

The position is now covered by s.125(1) of the Housing Act 1974. This allows the court a discretion to order specific performance of a landlord's repairing obligation, whether the alleged breach relates to a part of the premises let to the tenant or a part retained by the landlord, and despite any equitable rule, such as lack of mutuality, adequacy of damages or impossibility of supervision, which might otherwise have restricted the availability of this remedy. This jurisdiction can be exercised over an undertaking to repair, maintain, renew, construct or replace any property, and can be invoked by any tenant except one to whom Part II of the Landlord and Tenant Act 1954 applies (i.e. a tenant of premises which are occupied, at least in part, for business purposes.)

Section 125(1) is confined to repairing covenants relating to a dwelling, which is defined as a building or part of a building occupied or intended to be occupied as a separate dwelling, together with any yard, garden, outhouses and appurtenances belonging to or usually enjoyed with that building or part (s.129(1) H.A. 1974).

7. DEDUCTING THE COST OF REPAIRS FROM THE RENT

In *Lee-Parker* v. *Izzet* [1971] 1 W.L.R. 1688, GOFF J. revived 'an ancient common-law right' to deduct from rent any legitimate expenditure by the tenant on repairs which ought to have been done by the landlord. This right, which takes the form of a defence to an action for rent, or, presumably, to an action for possession for non-payment of rent, is confined to expenditure which, on the facts, it was proper for the tenant to incur. It arises only if the landlord is in breach of a repairing obligation. Hence, if the landlord is entitled to notice of defects before he can come under any obligation, such notice must have been given.

It remains to be seen whether this defence extends to deductions from the rent made in *anticipation* of expenditure by the tenant on repairs which the landlord has failed to execute.

CHAPTER 3

COMPULSORY IMPROVEMENT BY THE LOCAL AUTHORITY

Apart from the responsibilities of landlord and tenant for the state of the premises which they owe principally to each other, and which are enforceable, in the last resort, by action in the civil courts, occupiers or owners also owe a wider social or public duty for the state of their premises.

It falls to the local authority, generally speaking, to ensure that certain minimum standards are observed. The powers and duties of a local authority are drawn from various statutory provisions, and are sanctioned both by the criminal and the civil law. In this chapter, two sets of provisions designed to enable an authority to compel the improvement of dwellings will be examined: the provisions of Part II of the Housing Act 1957 and those of the Housing Act 1974.

1. Compulsory improvement under the Housing Act 1957

a. Powers and duties conferred on the local authority

Part II of the Housing Act 1957 contains provisions whereby a local authority can compel the repair or improvement of individual dwellings. These provisions are designed to secure that housing meets a minimum standard of fitness in respect of, but only in respect of, certain designated matters. These are listed in s.4, which is considered above, pp. 18–19.

The powers and duties under Part II are exercisable over any *house* in the local authority area. This includes any part of a building which is used, or is suitable for use, as a dwelling (s.18(1)(*a*) H.A. 1957); it also includes any hut, tent, caravan or other temporary or moveable shelter which is used for human habitation, provided it has been in the same enclosure for at least two years immediately preceding action by the local authority (ss.9(3), 16(7) H.A. 1957; *Benabo* v. *Wood Green B.C.* [1945] 2 All E.R. 162 (D.C.)).

By s.72 of the Housing Act 1969, these provisions now apply not only to a house which is unfit for human habitation according to the standard of s.4 of the 1957 Act, but also to one which, though fit by that standard, requires substantial repairs to put it into a reasonable state. The Act does not specify what constitutes a reasonable standard, so once more it is a question of the particular circumstances of each case. However, in deciding whether a house is of a reasonable standard, the local authority must have regard to its age, character and locality (s.9(1A) H.A. 1957).

b. Initiation of proceedings

Information that a house is in disrepair or is in some other respect inadequate, may be received by a local authority from an official or unofficial source. Official representations about the state of premises *must* be made by the medical officer of health if he is of the opinion that a particular house is unfit for human habitation. His opinion can be demanded by a Justice of the Peace, thus placing the medical officer of health under an immediate duty to inspect, and providing a means of starting proceedings more quickly than might otherwise have been the case (s.157(1), (2) H.A. 1957).

c. Determining the appropriate course of action

If a local authority is satisfied that a house is unfit according to s.4 of the 1957 Act, or that substantial repairs are required to put it into a reasonable state, it must take action. The particular action to be taken, and the procedure to be followed, depends upon whether the local authority believes that the house can be made fit at a reasonable expense. This decision must be based upon a comparison of the estimated cost of the necessary works with the estimated freehold value of the house when the works are done (s.39(1)), and must be made in an objective manner, without regard to any special circumstances affecting the individual against whom the local authority will act, (e.g. his financial condition) (*per* LORD EVERSHED M. R. in *Maurice (Leslie) & Co. Ltd* v. *Willesden Corporation* [1953] 2 Q.B. 1 at p. 5 (C.A.)).

The individual who will eventually be ordered to do the work has no right to be heard by the local authority at this stage (*per* SLESSER L. J. in *Johnson* v. *Leicester Corporation* [1934] 1 K.B. 638 at 646 (C.A.)).

d. Where the house can be made fit at a reasonable expense

i. *Service of notice*

Having decided that the house can be made fit at a reasonable expense, the local authority *must* serve a notice upon the person who has control of the house, i.e. the person who, either on his own behalf or as agent or trustee of another, receives the rackrent of the house, or who would receive it, were the house let at a rackrent. A rackrent is a rent which is at least two-thirds of the full net annual value of the house (s.39(2) H.A. 1957). The notice must:

(*a*) be in due form and signed by the clerk to the local authority or his lawful deputy (s.166(2) H.A. 1957). A facsimile signature suffices (*Plymouth City Corporation* v. *Hurrell* [1968] 1 Q.B. 455 (C.A.); *Graddage* v. *London Borough of Haringey* [1975] 1 All E.R. 224).

(*b*) specify in sufficient detail the works to be done (*per* MAUGHAM J. in *Cohen* v. *West Ham Corporation* [1933] Ch. 814 at 827–8).

(*c*) give the person served a reasonable time, and in any case not less than twenty-one days, in which to carry out the specified works. What constitutes a reasonable time is a question of individual circumstances.

(*d*) state that, in the opinion of the local authority, the specified works will make the house suitable for human habitation (s.9(1) H.A. 1957).

ii. *Appeal against notice*

The individual who is served with a valid notice may appeal against it to the County court within twenty-one days of service. If the notice is invalid, e.g. because it is not properly signed, it can be ignored. Moreover, an appeal against an invalid notice will not validate it (*Graddage* v. *London Borough of Haringey*, above).

On appeal, the County court judge may in his discretion, confirm, vary or quash the notice. He is not bound to cure defects which he may find in the notice, e.g. insufficient time allowed or wrong works specified, by varying it rather than quashing it (s.11 H.A. 1957; *Cochrane* v. *Chanctonbury R.D.C.* [1950] 2 All E.R. 1134 (C.A.)).

iii. *Purchase of the unfit house by the local authority*

If an appeal is allowed, on whatever grounds, the local authority is entitled to require the judge to decide whether or not the house is capable of being made fit for human habitation at a reasonable expense. If the judge, in allowing an appeal, has found (whether or not at the invitation of the local authority) that the house cannot be made fit at a reasonable expense, the local authority is empowered to buy it, either by agreement or compulsorily; if this power is exercised, the authority must, within a reasonable time, carry out all the works specified in the notice against which the appeal was brought (s.12(1), (3) H.A. 1957 and see *Hillingdon London Borough Council* v. *Cutler* [1968] 1 Q.B. 124 as to the time within which the work must be carried out).

iv. *Execution of the repairs by the local authority*

A local authority is empowered by s.10 to enter the unfit

house and carry out the specified works itself, if the person on whom the notice was served fails to comply with its requirements in time. No court order is required. (cf. the circumstances in which a local authority can abate a statutory nuisance under s.95(2) of the Public Health Act 1936, below, pp. 52–3.)

The time allowed for doing the work is the period specified in the notice or, if there has been an appeal, twenty-one days from the final determination of the appeal or such longer time as the court may allow. Any expenses which the local authority incurs in carrying out the work may be recovered from the person on whom the notice was served, or his principal or, if he is a trustee, from a beneficiary of that trust (s.10(3) H.A. 1957).

e. Where the house cannot be made fit at a reasonable expense

i. *Service of notice*

If the local authority is satisfied that the house is unfit, but that it cannot be brought up to the standard of s.4 at a reasonable expense, notice must be served upon the person who has control of the house, any owner, and any mortgagee, so far as it is practicable for the authority to ascertain who the mortgagees are. The notice must specify a time (not less than twenty-one days after service) at which the local authority intends to consider the future of the house. The persons served are entitled to be heard at that time (s.16(1), 2) H.A. 1957).

ii. *Powers of the local authority*

When the time comes, the local authority may:

(*a*) accept an undertaking from an owner or a mortgagee who has submitted prior written proposals concerning the house, that he will carry out works which will render the house fit for human habitation, within a specified time; or (*b*) accept an undertaking from the same persons that the house shall not be used for human habitation until the local authority is satisfied that it is fit, at which time they may withdraw the undertaking; or

(*c*) make a demolition order; or

(*d*) make a closing order; or

(*e*) purchase the house, if satisfied that it is, or can be made, capable of providing accommodation which is adequate for the time being.

iii. *Where the premises form part of a house or are an underground room*

If the premises in question are part only of a house, or are an underground room, the local authority must make a closing order, if an undertaking in respect of that part or that room is not accepted. An underground room is a room with a floor which is more than three feet below the nearest street level, or more than three feet below the level of any ground within nine feet of the room, and it is unfit for human habitation if its average height is less than seven feet, or it does not conform to local authority regulations with regard to ventilation, lighting, and protection against dampness, effluvia, or exhalation.

iv. *Appeal*

Any person aggrieved by a demolition or closing order, or a notice of intention to purchase, may appeal to the County court within twenty-one days of service of the order or notice (s.20(1) H.A. 1957). The judge may confirm, vary, or quash the order or notice, or he may accept in its stead an undertaking from any appellant who had submitted proposals for the carrying out of works to the house when originally notified by the local authority of the intention to consider its future (s.20(3) H.A. 1957).

v. *Demolition by the local authority*

If any demolition order is not obeyed, the local authority may demolish the house, and recoup the expenses from the owner.

2. Compulsory improvement under the Housing Act 1974

a. Standard amenities

The powers of a local authority under Part VIII of the Housing Act 1974 are directed towards securing the provision of so-called standard amenities in dwellings in the district. The provisions of Part VIII in this respect replace those of Part II of the Housing Act 1964.

The standard amenities are the following:

(*a*) A fixed bath or shower, which should be in a bathroom. Where this location is not reasonably practicable, but it is reasonably practicable for the bath or shower to have a hot and cold water supply, then it may be in any part of the dwelling other than a bedroom.

(*b*) A hot and cold water supply at a fixed bath or shower.

(*c*) A wash-hand basin.

(*d*) A hot and cold water supply at a wash-hand basin.

(*e*) A sink.

(*f*) A hot and cold water supply at a sink.

(*g*) A water-closet. If reasonably practicable, this must be in, and accessible from within, the dwelling, or, where the dwelling is part of a larger building, in that building and *readily* accessible from the dwelling. A lavatory in the basement is not sufficient for a third-floor flat.

b. Initiation of proceedings

Initiation of the procedure for compelling the relevant person to provide standard amenities varies according to whether or not the dwelling in question is within a general improvement area or housing action area. If the dwelling is in a general improvement area or housing action area a local authority can proceed on its own initiative (s.85 H.A. 1974). In other cases, it can act only after receiving written representations from an occupying tenant of the dwelling (s.89 H.A 1974). Otherwise, the procedure is basically the same.

c. Conditions to be satisfied before taking action

Before taking action, the local authority must be satisfied as to two matters: first, that the dwelling in question meets certain requirements, and, second, that it is capable of improvement up to one of two standards, at a reasonable expense.

i. *Condition and age of the dwelling*

The initial requirements which the dwelling must satisfy are as follows: first, the dwelling must lack one or more of the standard amenities, although it need not also be in a state of disrepair, and, second, it must have been provided, either by erection or conversion, *before* 3rd October 1961.

ii. *Improvement to the full or reduced standard*

The authority can proceed if satisfied that the dwelling can be improved up to the so-called full standard or, if that is not possible, up to the so-called reduced standard, at a reasonable expense. These standards are to be found in s.66(2) and (6).

A dwelling attains the full standard if it satisfies the following five requirements:

(*a*) it is provided with all the standard amenities, for the exclusive use of its occupants;

(*b*) it is in good repair, in view of its age, character and locality. Internal decorative repair is disregarded;

(*c*) it conforms to any specified central government requirements relating to thermal insulation which have been made for the purposes of s.66;

(*d*) it is in all other respects fit for human habitation, as that phrase is understood in s.4 H.A. 1957 (above, pp. 18–19).

(*e*) it is likely to be available for use as a dwelling for fifteen years, or such other period as may be specified by the central government under s.66.

The reduced standard is not fixed, but is anything less than the full standard. Under s.66(3) and (4) a local authority may dispense with any of the first four requirements, and under s.66(5) a shorter period during which the house is to be available as a dwelling may be substituted. For example, a dwelling might not be capable of improvement at a reasonable expense up to the full standard, but might nevertheless be improved at a reasonable expense so as to satisfy, say, items (*a*) and (*d*) of the above list, in which case the local authority may set this as the requisite reduced standard.

iii. *Additional requirements where the dwelling is outside a general improvement area or housing action area*

If the dwelling is outside a general improvement area or housing action area, the local authority must also be satisfied that the person from whom written representations were received is an occupying tenant of the deficient premises, that in all the circumstances the dwelling ought to be improved, and that it is unlikely that it will be improved unless the local authority exercises its powers.

An 'occupying tenant' is defined in s.104(1) as someone who is not an owner-occupier but who occupies or is entitled to occupy the dwelling as a lessee, or who is a statutory tenant, or who occupies under a Part VI contract (see below, pp. 96–98) or by virtue of being an agricultural employee.

d. Discretionary nature of powers

Even if the authority is satisfied as to all these matters, there is no *obligation* to proceed further, but if no action is taken the occupying tenant, in the case of a house outside a general improvement area or housing action area, is entitled to a written statement of the authority's reasons for its decision (s.89(4)(*b*) H.A. 1974).

e. Service of provisional notice

If it is decided to take action, the local authority must serve a provisional notice on the person who has control of the dwelling. He is defined in rather different terms from those used in the 1957 Act (see above, p. 34). For the purposes of Part VIII of the 1974 Act, the person having control of a dwelling is either:

(*a*) the owner-occupier, that is, an owner or a lessee under a long tenancy, who occupies, or is entitled to occupy the dwelling. A long tenancy is a tenancy for a term in excess of twenty-one years; or

(*b*) if the dwelling is occupied by an agricultural employee, the person by whose authority he occupies; or

(*c*) in any other case, the owner or lessee under a long tenancy (s.104(2) H.A. 1974).

A provisional notice cannot, however, be served on an owner-occupier unless the improvement of his dwelling is reasonably necessary in order to improve an adjacent dwelling, or a dwelling in the same building, which either is *not* owner-occupied, or for which an improvement, intermediate, special, or repairs grant has been approved under Part VII of the Housing Act 1974.

The notice must specify the works necessary to bring the dwelling up to the required standard, and state a time, place and date, not less than twenty-one days after service, at which the matter will be considered.

Copies of the notice must be sent to any occupying tenant, and anyone known to the local authority to be an owner, lessee, or mortgagee. All these persons are entitled to be heard.

f. Powers of the local authority

The local authority, after taking the views of these people into account, may:

(*a*) accept a written undertaking from the person who has control of the dwelling or anyone with an estate or interest in it, to improve the dwelling to the required standard. An undertaking can only be accepted if satisfactory arrangements have been made for accommodating any displaced tenant and that tenant has added his written consent to the undertaking (s.87 H.A. 1974).

(*b*) serve an improvement notice on the person who has control of the dwelling, if no undertaking has been accepted. Once again, the local authority must be satisfied that proper housing arrangements have been made for any occupying tenant who will be displaced in consequence of the works (s.88 H.A. 1974).

The person served, the occupying tenant, or anyone else with an estate or interest in the dwelling, may appeal to the County court within six weeks from service of an improvement notice (s.91 H.A. 1974).

If the specified works are not completed within the time allowed, they may be executed by the local authority itself, which can recover any reasonably incurred expenses from the person who has control of the dwelling (s.94 H.A. 1974).

The person on whom an improvement notice has been served has the right to enter the dwelling to inspect its condition and to carry out the specified works. Anyone who prevents him from carrying out the inspection or the works may be ordered by a magistrate to allow him to proceed unimpeded, and violation of such an order is a summary offence, punishable by a maximum fine of £20, (s.96(3) H.A. 1974, s.161 H.A. 1957).

The provisions of Part VIII do not apply where the person who has control of the dwelling is a local authority, or any other body listed in s.5(2) of the Rent Act 1968, as amended (see further below, p. 110).

3. Miscellaneous improvement powers

Local authorities possess other powers to compel the improvement or repair of certain types of dwelling in certain circumstances. These powers are culled from various Acts of Parliament, and fall into two general categories: powers in respect of houses in multiple occupation, which are considered in Chapter 5, and powers under Public Health legislation.

The most important powers (and duties) of a local authority in respect of their public health function are those given or imposed in ss.91–94 of the Public Health Act 1936 to control the incidence of so-called statutory nuisances. This subject is considered in the next chapter. Other public health powers include the following:

(*a*) Under s.39 of the Public Health Act 1936, a local authority can compel the owner of a building to provide it with satisfactory drainage, or to repair, renew, or cleanse any cesspool, private sewer, drain, soilpipe, rainwater pipe, spout, sink, or other appliance which is necessary for the drainage of the building.

Section 56 of the same Act empowers the local authority to require a houseowner to provide for the proper drainage of any yard, court, or passage giving access to the house.

Under s.18 of the Public Health Act 1961, the

local authority can repair a defective drain or private sewer if they estimate the cost of repair at £50 or below, and can recover the costs from the owner of the premises or the owner of the sewer.

(*b*) Under s.44 of the Public Health Act 1936, as amended, a local authority can compel the owner of a building to provide it with adequate toilets. The authority cannot require that these be water-closets rather than earth-closets, unless there is a sufficient water supply and sewer available, or unless the order is to replace an existing defective water-closet.

Under s.45 of the same Act, the local authority can direct that toilets which are in such a state as to be prejudicial to health or a nuisance be put into a satisfactory condition, by cleansing or otherwise.

Under s.40, the local authority can compel an owner or occupier to ensure that the wastepipes of water-closets are adequately ventilated, and that no rainwater pipe does double duty as a wastepipe from any sanitary convenience.

CHAPTER 4

STATUTORY NUISANCE

1. The 'cheap and speedy procedure'

The Public Health Act 1936 provides a mechanism for compelling the improvement of certain defective premises by means of summary proceedings in a Magistrates' court. This mechanism may be utilised both by local authorities and by private individuals who can show a sufficient grievance. The 'cheap and speedy procedure' which, according to Lord Goddard C.J. in *R.* v. *Epping (Waltham Abbey) Justices, ex parte Burlinson* [1948] K.B. 79, the Act provides, reflects the origin of local government involvement in housing conditions as an aspect of their public health function.

The relevant provisions of the Act, ss.91–99, relate to so-called statutory nuisances. These are defined in s.92. Sections 91, 93 and 94 specify the steps which a local authority should take to deal with them, and s.99 enables any aggrieved person to bring the same proceedings that the local authority might have brought.

2. What constitutes a statutory nuisance

a. Statutory provisions

Section 92(1) divides statutory nuisances into six categories and s.1 of the Noise Abatement Act 1960 adds a seventh. Of the original six, the first three and the last are relevant to our subject. These are:

(*a*) any premises in such a state as to be prejudicial to health or a nuisance;

(*b*) any animal kept in such a place or manner as to be prejudicial to health or a nuisance;

(*c*) any accumulation or deposit which is prejudicial to health or a nuisance;

(*d*) any other matter declared by any provision of this Act to be a nuisance. There are three such matters:

(*i*) any well, tank, cistern or water butt which is part of a domestic water supply and is so placed, constructed or kept as make the water liable to unhealthy contamination (s.141);

(*ii*) any pond, pool, gutter, ditch or watercourse which is in such a state as to be prejudicial to health or a nuisance, or any part of a watercourse not ordinarily navigated by goods vessels which is so blocked up as to produce conditions which are prejudicial to health or a nuisance (s.259(1)); and

(*iii*) any tent, van, shed or similar structure used for human habitation which is in such a state or so overcrowded as to be prejudicial to the health of its occupants, or the use of which gives rise to conditions which are prejudicial to health or a nuisance (e.g. by reason of inadequate sanitation) (s.268(2)).

The Noise Abatement Act 1960 adds to the list any noise or vibration which is a common law nuisance, but the procedure to be followed by private complainants (see below, pp. 53–60) is slightly different here from the procedure laid down in the parent Act, inasmuch as *three* aggrieved persons, who are also occupiers of land or premises, must jointly complain.

b. Difficulties of interpretation

Noise and vibration apart, it is apparently sufficient if the matter in question is *either* a nuisance *or* is prejudicial to health. Presumably the word 'nuisance' signifies a common law nuisance, i.e. an activity which constitutes an unreasonable and unjustified interference with someone's use and enjoyment of real property and which takes place outside that property, while the phrase 'prejudicial to health' relates to situations where there is no common law nuisance.

However, this straightforward interpretation of the Act is complicated by the case law. Two questions arise: to what extent, if any, must a common law nuisance also be prejudicial to health, in order for the Act to apply? In other words, ought one to assume that the nuisance provisions of a Public Health Act are necessarily confined to matters affecting the public health? And, second, if there is no common law nuisance because the matter complained of arises on premises occupied by the complainant, will a 'statutory nuisance' exist only where there is a threat to health?

The first question was considered by a divisional court in *Bishop Auckland Local Board* v. *Bishop Auckland Iron & Steel Co. Ltd* [1882] 10 Q.B.D. 138 in relation to s.91(4) of the Public Health Act 1875, the precursor of s.92(1)(*c*) of the 1936 Act. The matter complained of was an ashtip, which the respondents had allowed to accumulate on the site of their iron and steel works. The tip gave off a strong and offensive smell to neighbouring houses, but the complainants did not establish that this smell was actually injurious to health.

STEPHEN J. expressed the opinion that 'the words "nuisance or injurious to health" do not mean "nuisance injurious to health" . . . the natural sense of the words seems to me the best one to apply in the present case, i.e. a nuisance either interfering with personal comfort or injurious to health . . . I think the legislature intended to strike at anything which would diminish the comfort of life though not injurious to health and at anything which in fact would injure health'.

Provided a common law nuisance comes within these terms, therefore, it can probably be attacked through the statutory nuisance provisions of the 1936 Act. In any event, it is quite possible to argue that a nuisance which interferes with personal comfort, at least to a substantial degree, does threaten the mental, if not the physical, health and well-being of those affected by it.

However, in *Coventry City Council* v. *Cartwright* [1975] 2 All E.R. 99 (D.C.) Lord Widgery C.J. expressed the opinion that s.92 is directed towards situations with public health consequences. A refuse tip is therefore not a statutory nuisance merely because it is visually offensive. The court also ruled that an inert accumulation of rubbish is not a threat to *health* if it merely presents a danger of physical *injury* to those coming on to the site where it is located.

The second question represents the other side of the same coin. Must a state of affairs which would have been a common law nuisance, and a statutory nuisance within Stephen J's terms, but for the fact that it arises on premises which are occupied by the complainant, be actually prejudicial to his health, or is it sufficient that his personal comfort is diminished? The obvious answer would seem to be that it must, but the position is obscured somewhat by the controversial case of *Betts* v. *Penge U.D.C.* [1942] 2 K.B. 154.

The defendant in *Betts* was landlord of a flat occupied by a lady and her two children. She was holding over after notice to quit and was also in arrears of rent. Instead of applying to the County court for a possession order or for leave to distrain, the landlord took the law into his own hands by removing the front door and some window sashes. The local authority preferred a complaint of statutory nuisance against him for this blatantly anti-social behaviour, and the justices decided that he was guilty. It was sufficient in their opinion that his acts interfered with the personal comfort of the occupants, even though there was no finding that their health was endangered thereby. The defendant appealed. A divisional court, without reserving judgment, affirmed the magistrates' decision, in the belief that the *Bishop Auckland* case covered the situation.

It is doubtful whether this belief was justified. Stephen J's judgment, considered above, supports the proposition that a common law nuisance is actionable under the public health legislation if it interferes with personal comfort. This proviso in fact imposes a *limitation* upon the scope of summary proceedings for statutory nuisance, since it qualifies the phrase 'or a nuisance'. The *Penge* judgments support the inverse proposition: that any state of affairs which interferes with personal comfort is a nuisance for the purposes of the Public Health Act, whether or not it is also the common law tort. These judgments therefore considerably *widen* the scope of the phrase 'or a nuisance' beyond its common law meaning.

Betts v. *Penge U.D.C.* was distinguished by a later divisional court in *Springett* v. *Harold* [1954] 1 W.L.R. 521. A public health inspector preferred a complaint against a landlord under the Public Health (London) Act 1936 (since repealed). The cause of complaint was that the walls and ceilings in certain rooms let by the defendant were stained, dirty and peeling or flaking. There was no threat to the health of the inhabitants. The complaint was dismissed, on the ground that mere lack of decorative repair did not constitute a statutory nuisance, even if it was discomforting and inconvenient. On appeal by the inspector this decision was affirmed, LORD GODDARD C.J. thinking the case 'too clear for argument' and declining to give a judgment. It was felt sufficient to distinguish *Betts* v. *Penge U.D.C.* on the grounds that its facts 'were entirely different'.

It is hard to say just where these two cases leave the law. Perhaps one should return to the proposition that summary proceedings for statutory nuisance may be brought if *either* the premises in question are in a state prejudicial to health (as defined in the *Cartwright* case above) *or* there is a common law nuisance, involving at the least personal discomfort and perhaps the possibility of damage to health, but in no other circumstances.

3. DUTIES AND POWERS OF THE LOCAL AUTHORITY

A local authority has certain duties and powers in relation to statutory nuisances.

a. Inspection

First, it is the *duty* of every local authority, under s.91 of the Public Health Act 1936, to cause its district to be inspected from time to time for the detection of statutory nuisances. There is little that can be done by the private individual, however, should the local authority fail to carry out inspections. Furthermore, s.91 does not oblige the authority to *do* anything about nuisances which may be discovered; as will be seen, the position of local authorities with regard to the abatement of nuisances allows them some practical discretion whether to take action or not.

b. Abatement notices

The key provisions regarding abatement are to be found in sections 93 and 94. Section 93 requires a local authority to direct the person responsible for a nuisance to abate it, by serving a so-called abatement notice on him. However, this mandatory provision is predicated upon a proviso which takes out much of its obligatory quality. The duty to serve an abatement notice only arises where a local authority is satisfied that a statutory nuisance exists, and this decision need only be taken in good faith, and not upon reasonable grounds.

i. *On whom an abatement notice may be served*

Where the nuisance arises from any defect of a structural character, the person to be served with an abatement notice is the owner of the premises. It appears from the wording of s.93 that this is an absolute provision, even if it is apparent that some person other than the owner caused the nuisance to arise or continue. Furthermore, to compound the oddity, it seems that the person directly responsible cannot be joined as defendant under s.97, since that section (which allows the local authority to proceed against one or some or all of several potential defendants) only applies as between those whose acts or defaults have caused the nuisance. The owner of premises therefore appears to be in a worse position when he is not at fault, although frequently he *will* be responsible for the nuisance, by virtue of having failed to observe a covenant to repair (see e.g. s.32 H.A. 1961).

Where the nuisance derives from a non-structural source, then the person by whose act, default, or sufferance the nuisance arises or continues must be served. But, if that person cannot be found (i.e. it is not obvious who caused the nuisance (*Rhymney Iron Co.* v. *Gelligaer D.C.* [1917] 1 K.B. 589)), then the local authority may choose to proceed against either the owner or the occupier, or, in certain circumstances, to abate the nuisance themselves (see below, pp. 52–3).

ii. *The meaning of 'structural defect'*

In an earlier chapter and in a different context, we have noted the difficulties in ascertaining the scope of references to structure (see above, pp. 21–2).

No indication is given in the 1936 Act of the meaning of the phrase 'defect of a structural character' in the context of a statutory nuisance. Drawing on the analogy of s.32, Housing Act 1961, which implies a covenant into certain tenancies to keep the structure of the dwelling in repair, and also the installations for the supply of water, gas, and electricity, it might be said that the structure of a house does not include these installations. On this view, dangerously defective electrical wiring, damaged gas or water pipes, or a leaking toilet would not constitute structural defects.

On a wider view, however, it can be argued that the structure of a building comprehends all its permanent features. Moreover, the words 'of a structural character' may well suggest that it is enough that the defect relates to the structure, even though it is not a defect *in* the structure. Clearly, there is a quite wide grey area between defects which are obviously structural (e.g. a holed roof) and those which are obviously not (mere decorative disrepair, for example).

iii. *Summary proceedings*

If the person on whom an abatement notice has been served fails to comply with the terms of the notice, or does comply but the nuisance is nevertheless likely to recur, the local authority is then required, under s.94 of the Public Health Act 1936, to lay a complaint (or an information: *Northern Ireland Trailers Ltd* v. *Preston Corporation* [1972] 1 W.L.R. 203 (D.C.)), thus initiating summary proceedings in which the person responsible for the nuisance must be ordered by the court to abate it, and can be fined up to £20. Despite the apparently mandatory terms of s.94(1), a local authority is entitled to deal with a nuisance situation under any of its powers, if the end result is the same (*Nottingham C.D.C.* v. *Newton* [1974] 1 W.L.R. 923 (D.C.)).

In theory, therefore, there is a direct progression of duties laid upon a local authority: to inspect their district in order to discover statutory nuisances; to serve abatement notices on those deemed to be responsible; and, finally, to bring summary proceedings if the notice is not obeyed. In practice, however, many local authorities are reluctant to serve abatement notices, preferring instead to issue informal warnings, perhaps because they are loath to be drawn into legal proceedings of this kind or because they feel that it is pointless to proceed against an impecunious landlord, or because they prefer to deal with the matter under one of their other powers.

iv. *Abatement by the local authority*

If the local authority believes that unreasonable delay would be caused by following through the procedure set out in ss.93–5, the authority may bypass it and remedy the defects directly, by serving a notice on the person on whom an abatement notice could have been served, stating the authority's intention to abate the nuisance, and specifying the defects intended to be remedied. After nine days from notification the local authority may do the works, and can then recover the costs from the person served, provided that the court in which they seek to recover those expenses determines that the authority was justified in taking direct action (s.26 P.H.A. 1961).

The local authority may also bypass court proceedings and abate the nuisance itself in the case of a nuisance arising from a non-structural source, if satisfied that the owner and occupier is in no way responsible.

In practice, however, in this latter situation a local authority may well prefer to proceed under sections 9 or 10 of the Housing Act 1957 (see above, pp. 32–8) or under s.83 of the Public Health Act 1936 (which provides for the cleansing of filthy or verminous premises), since the costs of abatement can then be recovered. The principal advantages of acting under the statutory nuisance provisions, which are to have the sanction of a court order and to alleviate pressure on their own Public Works department, are lost when the authority by-passes the court and does the necessary work itself.

4. Action by a person aggrieved

Many residents associations, legal aid centres, and similar organisations have begun to look upon the statutory nuisance provisions of the Public Health Act 1936 as a potent force in the struggle for better housing conditions. While it is true that a complaint under s.99 of the 1936 Act is one of the more serviceable weapons in a somewhat makeshift armoury of private rights, nevertheless a degree of circumspection must attend its use. A number of uncertainties and qualifications still lie around s.99, which may dull its edge. At all events, it has yet to be shown as the instrument with which to slice through the Gordian knot of present-day slum housing conditions. A closer examination of s.99 reveals the problems, as well as the potential, of this procedure.

a. 'The like proceedings'

Section 99, substantially re-enacting s.105 of the Public Health Act 1875, entitles any person aggrieved to bring a complaint of statutory nuisance before a magistrate, whereupon 'the like proceedings shall be had, with the like incidents and consequences as to the making of orders, penalties for disobedience of orders and otherwise, as in the case of a complaint by the local authority. . . .'

There is no indication in the Act that the local authority must first be given an opportunity of exercising its own powers to deal with the nuisance before s.99 proceedings can be initiated.

b. Difficulties of interpretation

i. *Generally*

The immediate difficulty is one of interpretation. The wording of the section makes it necessary to read its provisions back into the relevant parts of the preceding sections, in order to determine just what 'the like proceedings' are. All the prior sections dealing with statutory nuisance, however, are built upon the assumption that the local authority is, or will be, the complainant, but in a s.99 complaint the local authority may well be the defendant, or one of the defendants. Moreover, as we have seen, certain preliminary duties are imposed upon the local authority in these prior sections which are not imposed upon the private complainant, but which nevertheless are dovetailed into the actual complaint procedure. Thus, the sections which precede s.99, when read in this light, take on an awkward and unwieldy aspect. It is not clear when one can read 'person aggrieved' for 'local authority' and when not.

ii. *Relevance of abatement notice procedure*

This is particularly apparent with regard to s.93. This section fulfills two functions: first, it requires a local authority to serve an abatement notice, when satisfied of the existence of a statutory nuisance, and, second, it nominates the persons on whom that notice can be served. If the terms of the notice are not obeyed, the local authority is required by s.94 to bring summary proceedings against those persons to whom the notice was directed. Thus s.93 identifies, albeit indirectly, the potential defendants to a complaint by the local authority.

Under s.99, however, there is no requirement that the aggrieved person first serve an abatement notice. The provisions of s.93 and s.94 are therefore not directly relevant, and no straightforward means is provided for ascertaining the defendants in a private action.

The question of whether an abatement notice must be served as a preliminary to a private complaint was considered by a divisional court in *Cocker* v. *Cardwell* (1869) 5 Q.B. 15, in relation to s.13 of the Nuisances Removal Act 1860, a precursor to s.99. Two members of the court regarded the absence of such a requirement as a legislative oversight. Be this as it may, neither s.105 of the Public Health Act 1875, nor s.99 of the 1936 Act, introduced this condition. As a matter of statutory construction it seems unarguable that no abatement notice need precede a s.99 complaint. The problem of harmonising s.99 with ss.93 and 94 remains.

Is one left to assume, therefore, that the appropriate defendants to a s.99 complaint are those identified, however clumsily, in s.93, and, moreover, that this comprehends the local authority itself? Should a sub-tenant proceed against his landlord or against the owner of the premises? The overlay of s.99 upon other sections drafted with different ends in view is not a particularly satisfactory method of indicating the rights of the private complainant, or the steps he must take to enforce those rights.

c. The complainant

Any 'person aggrieved' may institute summary proceedings for the abatement of a statutory nuisance. The meaning of this familiar legislative phrase has not yet been considered by the courts in the context of s.99, but one may assume that it does not comprehend the individual whose social sensibilities alone are offended, who may feel a sense of grievance as that phrase is popularly understood. Hence the public-minded citizen has no standing to make a complaint, although, in earlier legislation, the *inhabitants* of a local authority area were given the right to bring proceedings, as well as those actually aggrieved.

It is not clear whether the complainant must show that a distinct private right has been violated to qualify as an aggrieved person, or whether it is sufficient that he has some general interest in the affected premises. Is it enough, for example, for a complainant to establish that he is an occupant of the relevant premises, and that they are in a state prejudicial to his health, or must he establish that he is a tenant or licensee and that the state of the premises constitutes the breach of some provision in the lease or licence? It is not unknown for magistrates' clerks to reject a complaint signed by a tenant's wife rather than the tenant himself.

The phrase 'person aggrieved' appears frequently, in many different kinds of legislation. Until quite recently, courts had tended to follow the lead of JAMES L.J. who, in *In re Sidebotham* (1880) 14 Ch. D. 458 (a bankruptcy case) gave the words a restrictive interpretation. He suggested that a person is only aggrieved if his private rights have been infringed by the matter in question. This attitude has subsequently revealed itself in issues as diverse as that of standing to appeal against a grant of planning permission (*Buxton* v. *M.H.L.G.* [1961] 1 Q.B. 278; *Gregory* v. *Camden London Borough Council* [1966] 1 W.L.R. 899) and the obligation of a private individual to provide a dustbin, under s.75 of the Public Health Act 1936 (*R.* v. *Nottingham Quarter Sessions, ex parte Harlow* [1952] 2 Q.B. 601 (D.C.)).

The tendency of more recent cases, however, some of which are reviewed by ACKNER J. in *Turner* v. *Secretary of State for the Environment* [1973] 72 L.G.R. 380, is to give standing to those who have a legitimate interest in the particular matter, even though they may not have a legal grievance in the strict sense. A legitimate interest is an interest beyond that of an ordinary member of the public.

It is difficult to predict whether a s.99 complainant could be drawn within the aegis of these more liberal decisions. The precise scope which a court gives to the phrase 'person aggrieved' depends upon its particular statutory context and perhaps even upon the nature of the relief sought (see *per* LORD HEWART C.J. in *Sevenoaks U.D.C.* v. *Twynam* [1929] 2 K.B. 440). It is therefore quite possible that the same phrase may have different meanings in different statutes, or even in different parts of the same Act. Although the *Sidebotham* interpretation has been modified in cases on planning legislation, it has yet to be called in question in the context of s.99 of the Public Health Act 1936.

d. The defendant

i. *The local authority as defendant*

It is now generally supposed that a local authority can be made defendant under s.99 if it fails to take action to abate a nuisance, although, from the wording of the Act, this liability is far from obvious. The unreserved judgment of LORD GODDARD C.J. in *R.* v. *Epping (Waltham Abbey) Justices, ex parte Burlinson* [1948] K.B. 79 provides the rather tenuous basis on which the supposition rests.

The particular point at issue in *Burlinson's* case was whether a local authority could be made defendant to a s.99 complaint when the nuisance had been created by the authority itself. It was decided that this was possible. It seems, moreover, from a careful reading of the principal judgment, that LORD GODDARD C.J. was confining his attention to this situation, and there is little to suggest that a s.99 complaint can be directed against a local authority simply because its own powers of abatement have not been exercised.

LORD GODDARD C.J. accepted the complainant's submission that s.99 applies in two situations: where it is alleged that the local authority has not carried out its own duty, and where the local authority itself is alleged to have caused the nuisance. The first of these situations, however, simply indicates that a private individual can complain against *the person responsible* for the nuisance, if the local authority has failed to do so, not that he can complain against the authority directly. Of course, in this situation the court can order the local authority to abate the nuisance, having first allowed the authority the opportunity to be heard, but this does not mean that the authority is directly amenable to a s.99 complaint.

The only other peg on which to hang a complaint against the authority is that the authority itself has somehow caused the nuisance. In the course of his judgment, LORD GODDARD

C.J. asserted that 'where a nuisance exists it is the duty of the local authority to take proceedings for the abatement of the nuisance'. It is doubtful, however, whether he meant to suggest that a breach of this duty alone would render the authority liable under s.99 for having caused the nuisance. It seems more likely that he was concerned to establish the two separate points: that if the authority has failed to proceed, the aggrieved individual may do so, and that, if the authority is itself causing the nuisance, the authority is liable under s.99 to the same extent as any other responsible party.

Even if LORD GODDARD C.J.'s dictum is interpreted in the manner least favourable to local authorities, two caveats must be entered against it. First, a *duty* to take proceedings arises only where the local authority is satisfied of the existence of a statutory nuisance. Second, it is doubtful whether a local authority can be said to cause a nuisance by failing to invoke its own powers to have the nuisance abated. In such circumstances can it be said that the nuisance arises or continues by the authority's act, default, or sufferance? These words connote the breach of some duty, but, as has been noted, no clear duty arises without the authority's own fiat.

The case might be stronger if the authority could be required to abate the nuisance in default of the party principally responsible doing so. But, although an authority has the *power* to do this under s.95(2), there is no *duty* to act, if the person ordered by the court to abate the nuisance fails to obey. Hence, even if a local authority does instigate abatement proceedings, there is no certainty that the nuisance will be stopped.

Be this as it may, the point is not one that local authorities appear to take in their own defence. In *Nottingham C.D.C.* v. *Newton* [1974] 1 W.L.R. 923 (D.C.) the local authority, joined as defendants with a landlord, did not dispute liability on this ground, but raised a different defence. Both the Corporation and the landlord contested the complaint, and then appealed against the magistrates' order, on the ground that the house in question was in a slum clearance area and subject to an unconfirmed compulsory purchase order.

Since it was expected that the order would be confirmed within a few months, and the premises demolished soon afterwards, the defendants argued that any expenditure on the house would be pointless. They suggested that magistrates have a discretion whether or not to issue a nuisance order, and invited the bench to exercise this discretion on their behalf. The decision of the divisional court makes clear that there is no such discretion. Once it is established that a nuisance exists, the magistrates *must* make a nuisance order.

Although LORD WIDGERY C.J. agreed that the defendants' contention was a sensible one, he refused to accede to it, and decided instead that magistrates should take account of all the circumstances when fixing the terms of their order. Justices do have a discretion in setting the time by which the nuisance must be removed, and can also specify a programme for doing the necessary work. Hence they should bear in mind the likelihood or imminence of demolition when detailing their order. In case justices are inclined to lean too far in this direction, however, it should be remembered that the function of the statutory nuisance procedure is to provide a speedy remedy for those whose health is endangered by the condition of defective premises. Occupants should not be required to live in unhealthy conditions simply because their home is scheduled for demolition at some time in the future, but provided the nuisance is abated quickly, there is no reason why the standard of repair should not reflect the life expectancy of the premises (cf. s.32(3) H.A. 1961).

It remains to be seen whether a new line of defence will succeed. In *Salford City Council* v. *McNally* [1975] 1 All E.R. 597 a local authority had acquired premises in a clearance area and, believing them to be of an adequate standard for the time being, continued to use them to provide accommodation, as a local authority is entitled to do by s.48(1) H.A. 1957. A tenant of one such house succeeded in obtaining a nuisance order against the local authority. An appeal to the divisional court, on the ground that s.48(1) qualified the obligations of the local authority under the Public Health Act 1936, was dismissed. At the time of writing, an appeal to the House of Lords is pending.

ii. *Other defendants*

A s.99 complaint may be brought against other defendants than the local authority. Since an aggrieved person is entitled to bring the like proceedings to those which the authority might have brought, it is arguable that the appropriate defendants to a private action are those nominated in ss.93 and 94, namely the owner if the nuisance has a structural source, and the person causing the nuisance in all other cases. This should be so whether or not the circumstances also constitute a breach of some agreement between the complainant and the defendant or a third party.

It should be noted, finally, that the statutory nuisance procedure of the Public Health Act 1936 is not a means of ensuring that landlords provide their tenants with a fit place to live, but merely that it should not be unhealthy.

CHAPTER 5

OVERCROWDING AND MULTIPLE OCCUPATION

1. Generally

Overcrowding is one of the commonest, and most acute, symptoms of housing stress. The law, which cannot yet ensure that everyone who needs one has a home of his own, attempts to meet the problem of overcrowding in part by penalising its occurrence. Thus it is, generally speaking, a criminal offence to allow premises to become overcrowded. However, the law in this area should be seen in the context of those other measures which deal with the provision of housing and its compulsory improvement, as part of the overall method by which local authorities attempt to cope with the housing problem.

There are two different sets of statutory provisions which are relevant to overcrowding. These deal with, first, overcrowding in separate dwelling-units, and, second, overcrowding in premises occupied by persons who do not form a single household (i.e. houses in multiple occupation). Anyone who occupies a separate dwelling in premises that house more than one family will probably be subject to both sets of provisions.

2. Overcrowding in a separate dwelling-unit

a. The meaning of 'separate dwelling-unit'

i. *Statutory definition*

Section 77 of the Housing Act 1957, which defines overcrowding in relation to this first category, refers to a 'dwelling house'; this is defined in s.87 to mean any premises used as a separate dwelling by members of the working classes or of a type suitable for such use. The provisions discussed here are therefore concerned with separate homes, not separate houses in a structural sense. It is difficult to know what significance to attach to the reference to the working classes. In a different context, a police superintendent has been said not to be a member of the working class (*Rodway* v. *Minister of Health* [1947] K.B. 404) but it is perhaps better to adopt the view of DENNING J. that there is now no such separate class as the working class (*Green H.E. & Sons* v. *Minister of Health* [1948] 1 K.B. 34).

ii. '*Living Accommodation*'

It is not necessary that an occupant should have exclusive use of a complete set of rooms, with all essential facilities, in order for him to be in occupation of a separate dwelling. It is only necessary that he does not share any living accommodation with another household. The occupant's room or rooms still constitute a separate dwelling even if, for example, he lacks kitchen facilities and so must eat in cafeterias. But he would not have a separate dwelling if he shared a kitchen with someone else, because a kitchen is generally regarded as living accommodation.

If a living room is shared, then the premises are not a separate dwelling, even though the occupant may have exclusive possession of all his other rooms. If what might be called an occasional room alone is shared, then the rooms of which the occupant does have exclusive possession will constitute a separate dwelling.

An occasional room is one which is visited from time to time and for a specific purpose only, rather than a room in which the occupant can be said to live. This distinction was considered by the House of Lords in *Goodrich* v. *Paisner* [1957] A.C. 65, where the relevant authorities were reviewed.

Certain judicial opinions as to what constitutes a living room appear to be based upon the idea that a room can be classified, once and for all, according to its principal function.

Thus cooking, sleeping, and eating are, among others, regarded as 'essential manifestations of living' (see *per* LORD EVERSHED M.R. in *Hayward* v. *Marshall* [1952] 2 Q.B. 89 (C.A.)), while washing and visiting the lavatory apparently are not. For this reason it was decided in *Winters* v. *Dance* [1949] L.J.R. 165 (C.A.) that the sharing of a kitchenette, too small to do anything but cook in, nevertheless prevented the tenant from having a separate dwelling. On this view, none of the following is living accommodation: a bathroom, w.c., garage, cellar, attic, potting-shed, or laundry-room.

Perhaps, however, it is preferable to avoid a mechanical test, and to look instead at the facts of each particular case. Suppose, to take LORD RADCLIFFE'S example in *Goodrich* v. *Paisner* (above), that 'a single room in a small house is let unfurnished with the right to share the landlord's meals in the landlord's dining room. I would have said that the single room was not let as a single dwelling. On the other hand, the decision might be different if there was a common room in which meals were provided for the tenants of a number of one-roomed flats with their own front doors'. On this approach, the small kitchen might not count as a living room, if it could only be used for cooking.

iii. *Sharing*

One must also have regard to the nature and extent of the alleged sharing. If only a limited right to use a living room is allowed, this might not, in the circumstances, be sufficient to amount to sharing. This will be the case whether the occupant of the premises in question is given the limited use of a particular living room, or whether an outsider is allowed limited access to a room used principally by that occupant.

In *Hayward* v. *Marshall* (above) a landlord let three unfurnished rooms, and in addition gave his tenant the right to draw water from the landlord's kitchen and the right to boil his washing in the kitchen once a week. The Court of Appeal decided that the tenant nevertheless occupied his three rooms as a separate dwelling.

There are two possible explanations of this decision, however. There was no sharing in *Hayward's* case *either* because the permitted use was not sufficiently extensive, *or* because the tenant was not permitted to use the kitchen *as a kitchen*. The drawing of water and the boiling of clothes are not functions of a kitchen as such; one can do these things equally well elsewhere. On this view, if the tenant had been allowed to make a meal in the kitchen once a week there would then have been sharing.

b. The criteria of overcrowding in a separate dwelling-unit

There are three separate standards laid down in s.77 of the Housing Act 1957; each standard relates to the number of people who regularly sleep in the dwelling, and is confined to rooms which are suitable for that purpose.

A separate dwelling is overcrowded if the number of persons sleeping in the dwelling:

(*a*) is such that any two of those persons *must* sleep in the same room, and they are ten years old or more, of opposite sexes, and not living together as man and wife; or

(*b*) exceeds the permitted maximum number of persons who may sleep in a dwelling, calculated according to the *number* of sleeping rooms in the dwelling (see below); or

(*c*) exceeds the permitted maximum number of persons who may sleep in a room, calculated according to the *floor area* of those rooms.

It is not clear whether the first standard would be satisfied where a husband and wife sleep in one bedroom of a two-bedroom dwelling, and a son and daughter over the relevant age sleep in the other. On the strict wording of s.77(1)(*a*) it is, since both males *could* sleep in one room and both females in the other. It would no doubt be proper to take this strict view should this family be prosecuted, or threatened with loss of security of tenure under s.17 of the Rent Act 1968 (see below), particularly since s.77 is a criminal provision. It would be less justifiable for a local authority to adopt such an approach when fulfilling its statutory duty to give reasonable preference in the allocation of council tenancies to those who are living in overcrowded conditions.

The formulae for applying the second and third tests above can be found in the Sixth Schedule to the Housing Act 1957, which gives the maximum number of persons who may sleep in a house according to the number of rooms, and the maximum number who may sleep in a room, according to the floor area as follows:

Table I

Where a house consists of:

(*a*) One room .. .. 2 persons

(*b*) Two rooms .. .. 3 persons

(*c*) Three rooms .. .. 5 persons

(*d*) Four rooms .. .. 7½ persons

(*e*) Five rooms or more .. 10 persons, with an additional two persons in respect of each room in excess of five.

Table II

Where the floor area of a room is:

(*a*) 110 square feet or more: 2 persons

(*b*) 90 square feet or more, but less than 110 square feet: 1½ persons

(*c*) 70 square feet or more, but less than 90 square feet: 1 person

(*d*) 50 square feet or more, but less than 70 square feet: ½ person

(*e*) Under 50 square feet: Nil.

When applying Table I, no account is taken of any room with a floor area of less than fifty square feet.

When applying any of the three standards, two further considerations are relevant. First, no account is taken of a child under one year old, and a child who has attained one year but is less than ten years old is reckoned as half a unit (s.77(2) H.A. 1957). Second, no overcrowding offence is committed where the persons sleeping in an overcrowded dwelling include a member of the occupier's family who does not live there but is sleeping there temporarily, unless an overcrowding offence would be committed even if that person were not sleeping there (s.78(4) H.A. 1957). It would seem that an offence is committed if the temporary sleeper is not a member of the occupier's family.

c. The offence of overcrowding

A landlord is deemed to cause or permit overcrowding in two situations only:

(*a*) if, after notice in writing has been served upon the landlord or his agent by the local authority that the dwelling is overcrowded in such circumstances as to render the *occupier* guilty of an offence, the landlord fails to take such steps as are reasonably open to him for securing the abatement of the overcrowding, including, if necessary, legal proceedings for possession of the house; or

(*b*) if, when letting the house, the landlord (or any person effecting the letting on his behalf) had reasonable cause to believe that it would become overcrowded in such circumstances as to render the proposed occupier guilty of an offence, and failed to make inquiries of the proposed occupier as to the number, age, and sex of persons who would be allowed to sleep in the house (s.78(5) H.A. 1957).

An occupier does not commit an offence if the dwelling is

only overcrowded because a child has reached the age to be counted as a full or half unit, provided that the following conditions are satisfied:

(*a*) the occupier applies to the local authority to be rehoused (unless he has already applied before the child's birthday, in which case he need not re-apply).

(*b*) he does not refuse suitable alternative accommodation, should it be offered.

'Suitable alternative accommodation' is a dwelling-house in which the occupier and his family can live without being overcrowded, and which is certified by the local authority as being suitable to the needs of the occupier and his family in respect of security of tenure, proximity to work, and otherwise, and to be within his means (s.87 H.A. 1957).

(*c*) he directs any person who is not a member of his family to quit the dwelling, as and when practicable.

This defence is only available so long as all the persons sleeping in the house were living there at the child's birthday and continue to live there, or are children born to any such person (s.78(3) H.A. 1957).

d. Duty to notify the local authority

It is the duty of the landlord of an overcrowded dwelling to notify the local authority within a week of discovering that it is overcrowded, unless the authority already knows. Failure to notify is a summary offence punishable by a fine not exceeding £2 (s.83 H.A. 1957).

e. Proceedings and penalties

The local authority alone is empowered to bring proceedings

under the overcrowding provisions of the 1957 Act, but a prosecution can be brought *against* the local authority with the consent of the Attorney General (s.85(1) H.A. 1957).

The landlord or the occupier who causes or permits a dwelling-house to be overcrowded commits a summary offence, punishable by a maximum fine of £5, and a further fine of up to £2 for every day after conviction on which the offence continues (s.78(1) H.A. 1957).

f. Licensing of overcrowding

The local authority may licence an occupier or intending occupier to exceed the permitted number of occupants if the authority regards this as expedient in the light of exceptional circumstances. A licence may be conditional or unconditional, and although it may be granted for up to twelve months, it can nevertheless be revoked during its currency at the local authority's discretion. A period of grace of not less than one month from the date on which notice of revocation is served must be allowed, however (s.80 H.A. 1957).

g. Consequences of overcrowding

The tenant of a separate dwelling who commits an offence under s.78 above loses the protection of Part II of the Rent Act 1968, which gives security of tenure to protected and statutory tenants (see below, pp. 107–25). His landlord is therefore free to recover possession on any ground which would have been available to him but for the statutory shield, e.g. by serving a valid notice to quit premises let on a periodic tenancy. The offence of overcrowding does not *provide* a ground for recovering possession: it simply lifts the shield of the 1968 Act which was protecting the tenant (s.17 R.A. 1968). The landlord may only recover possession while the tenant is committing an offence, and this must be determined as at the time when the landlord's claim for possession is heard (*Zbytniewski* v. *Broughton* [1956] 2 Q.B. 673 (C.A.)).

The local authority itself can obtain a possession order from a *magistrates'* court in favour of the landlord. In order for this to be possible, the following must be shown:

(*a*) The authority must have served a notice on the occupier of a dwelling which was overcrowded in circumstances rendering him guilty of an offence, requiring him to abate the overcrowding within fourteen days of service of the notice.

(*b*) The dwelling must thereafter have been overcrowded, in such circumstances as to render the occupier guilty of an offence, at some time within a period of three months after expiry of the fourteen days.

(*c*) The dwelling must have been occupied during the three month period either by the person on whom the notice was served or a member of his family (s.85(2) H.A. 1957).

h. Rent book notices

A landlord must include in the rent book a summary of s.77 (the definition of overcrowding in separate dwellings), s.78 (the circumstances in which overcrowding is an offence) and s.80 (the power of a local authority to license overcrowding). In addition, the rent book must specify the permitted maximum number for the dwelling. Failure to include these items is a summary offence punishable by a fine of up to £10 (s.83 H.A. 1957).

3. Overcrowding in houses in multiple occupation

a. The meaning of a 'house in multiple occupation'

Unlike the preceding provisions, those about to be considered apply to houses in a structural sense. A house in multiple occupation is one which is occupied by persons who do not form a single household (s.90 H.A. 1957, as amended by s.58(1) H.A. 1969).

i. '*House*'

Section 90 of the Housing Act 1957 lays down the circumstances in which the offence of overcrowding in a multi-occupied dwelling will be committed. The scope of s.90 was considered by the Court of Appeal in *Reed* v. *Hastings Corporation* (1964) 62 L.G.R. 588 on the following facts: the appellant owned premises consisting of twelve large rooms, which he adapted to be used as a hostel for foreign schoolchildren during the summer, accommodating as many as ninety of them at any one time. There were adequate dining and sanitary facilities for such a number, but the local authority nevertheless took the view that it was too many. They therefore imposed a maximum of fifty, pursuant to their powers under s.90(1).

The owner appealed to the County court, which fixed upon seventy-three as the proper number. The owner, while accepting this figure, appealed again on the ground, inter alia, that his premises were not a 'house' within the meaning of s.90. The Court of Appeal took the view, in HARMAN L.J.'s words, that 'as a matter of policy, the local authority should . . . be empowered to control the density of population of any structure in their area used for the purposes of human habitation,' On this wide view, s.90 would seem to cover any structure, whether adapted or purpose-built, and whether used permanently or temporarily, in which people of more than one household can be said to live.

The scope of s.90 is arguably more limited, however. Part II of the Housing Act 1961 also contains provisions relating to houses in multiple occupation. Section 21 extends certain of these provisions 'to a building which is not a house but comprises separate dwellings. . . .' This suggests that 'house' signifies a building which was originally designed as separate residential accommodation for a single family. If this is the case, s.90 H.A. 1957 and the other statutory provisions about to be considered will not apply to any structure which was divided by original design into separate dwellings, e.g. a purpose-built block of flats.

On the other hand, it is established that a building which

was originally a single dwelling but has since been converted into separate and self-contained units remains a house, for the purposes of these provisions (*Okerere* v. *Brent London Borough Council* [1967] 1 Q.B. 42 (C.A.)).

ii. '*Single household*'

As s.90 was originally worded, it applied to houses occupied by members of more than one *family*. The second ground of appeal in *Reed's* case was that the premises in question, whether or not a house, were not being used by members of more than one family. This contention was also rejected, because 'family' connotes some blood tie, or at least some permanent domestic relationship.

It is arguable, however, that persons who come together to form a community, albeit for a short time or a temporary purpose can, in certain circumstances, form a single *household*, e.g. a boarding-school dormitory.

b. The offence of overcrowding in a multi-occupied house

i. *Notice by the local authority*

Unlike the position with regard to separate dwellings, it is not automatically an offence to cause or permit overcrowding in, or in part of, a house in multiple occupation. It is only an offence if the local authority serves a notice under s.90(1) on either a particular occupier or a person having control and management of the premises, or both, and thereafter the circumstances envisaged in s.90(4) arise.

The notice must state two things:

(*a*) the maximum number which the authority considers suitable for sleeping in any specified room (or, alternatively, that a specified room is unsuitable as sleeping accommodation) and

(*b*) the effect of subs. 4 of s.90, which specifies the

circumstances in which an offence will be committed, after a notice has become operative. The offence is committed if the person on whom the notice was served either:

(*i*) causes or knowingly permits any room to which the notice relates to be occupied as sleeping accommodation otherwise than in accordance with the notice; or

(*ii*) causes or knowingly permits to be accommodated on the premises such a number of persons that it is not possible to avoid persons of opposite sexes and over the age of twelve years (other than persons living together as husband and wife) occupying sleeping accommodation in the same room, without exceeding the permitted number in a specified room or utilising an unspecified room as sleeping accommodation.

If the room in question is, or is part of, a separate dwelling, the three s.77 standards must also be satisfied (see above, p. 64).

ii. *Appeal against notice*

A notice becomes operative after twenty-one days from service. Any person aggrieved by the notice may appeal against it, within those twenty-one days, to the County court. If the notice is confirmed, it becomes operative as from the date of final determination of the appeal (s.37(1) H.A. 1957).

iii. *Lapse of notice*

A notice is served on the person, not on the house, and so lapses with a change of occupation or control, as the case may be. And, since the notice relates to a house in multiple occupation, no offence can be committed by violating the terms of a notice after the house ceases to be multi-occupied (*Wolkind* v. *Ali* [1975] 1 All E.R. 193 (C.A.)).

c. Consequencies of overcrowding

Only the person served commits an offence, and he cannot lose his security of tenure because of it, since s.17(1) of the Rent Act 1968 is confined to offences of overcrowding in a separate dwelling. It will be recalled, however, that both s.78 and s.90 apply to a single separate dwelling in a multi-occupied house.

d. Penalties

The penalties for violation of a s.90 notice are now laid down in s.20 of the Housing Act 1961. These are a fine of up to £100 for a first conviction, and a fine of up to £100, or three months' imprisonment, or both, for a second or subsequent conviction.

4. Compulsory improvement of houses in multiple occupation

Sections 15 and 19 of the Housing Act 1961 and s.67 of the Housing Act 1964 form an important set of provisions, and should be considered together. They give a local authority certain powers over a house in multiple occupation which has inadequate facilities for the number of individuals or households living there, (and, incidentally, introduce a fourth criterion of overcrowding).

a. Improvement to accommodate the existing number of occupants

i. *Circumstances in which improvement can be ordered*

By virtue of s.15, a local authority can order the improvement of houses in multiple occupation which are, in the authority's opinion, unsuitable for occupation by the number of individuals or households presently there, because the house is inadequate for such a number in respect of any of the following amenities:

(*a*) Natural and artificial lighting;

(*b*) Ventilation;

(*c*) water supply;

(*d*) personal washing facilities;

(*e*) drainage and sanitary conveniences;

(*f*) facilities for the storage, preparation, and cooking of food, and for the disposal of waste water;

(*g*) installations for space heating or for the use of space heating appliances.

As we have already briefly noted, s.21 H.A. 1961 applies s.15, among others, to a building which is not a house but comprises separate dwellings, provided two or more of those dwellings are occupied by more than one household, or two or more of those dwellings do not have a sanitary convenience and personal washing facilities which are accessible only to those living in the particular dwelling.

ii. *Improvement notices*

The person served with a notice under s.15 must bring the premises up to a reasonable standard for the present number of occupants within the time specified in the notice, which must be at least three weeks. The particular works required in order to meet the requisite standard depend upon the circumstances of the particular case. Whether the provision of adequate personal washing facilities includes a piped supply of hot water is such a question (*McPhail* v. *Islington London Borough Council* [1970] 2 Q.B. 197 (C.A.)).

The necessary work must be done within the time specified in the notice (although the local authority may grant an extension of time) or, if an appeal is brought (see below, p. 75) and the notice confirmed, within twenty-eight days of confirmation, or such other time as the court may determine. Furthermore, the obligation to carry out the improvements continues, notwithstanding that the time specified in the notice or the time for appeal has passed, and notwithstanding conviction for having failed wilfully to comply with the terms of the notice (see below).

The local authority can serve a s.15 notice on either:

(*a*) the person who receives the rackrent (whether as principal, agent, or trustee) or who would receive it, were the premises let at a rackrent, and who is therefore deemed to have control of the house; or

(*b*) anyone to whom the house is let at a rackrent, or any agent or trustee of such a person who receives rents or other payments from tenants of parts of the house or lodgers in the house.

An appeal against a s.15 notice lies to the County court within twenty-one days of service, on the grounds specified in s.17 H.A. 1961, viz: that the notice was not justified in view of the condition of the house and the numbers accommodated there; that the notice was formally defective; that insufficient time for doing the work was allowed; that the works required were unreasonable or that a scheme of alternative improvements was unreasonably rejected by the authority; or that the wrong person was served.

The penalties for failing to comply with a s.15 notice are laid down in s.65(1) of the Housing Act 1964 and s.61(2) of the Housing Act 1969. It is a summary offence to fail wilfully to comply with the notice, punishable on first conviction by a fine of up to £100, and on subsequent conviction by a fine of up to £100, or three months' imprisonment, or both.

It is an additional offence, punishable by a fine of up to £100, to fail wilfully to execute the works after the time limit allowed has passed (s.61(1) H.A. 1969).

iii. *Execution of the improvements by the local authority*

If the terms of the notice are not complied with, the local authority may do the work, recovering the cost from the person served with the notice, or his principal. By virtue of the general provision in s.158 of the Housing Act 1957, the authority can, if necessary in order to do the work, obtain possession of the premises, regardless of the Rent Act 1968.

b. Power to impose maximum number of individuals or households

i. *Circumstances in which a maximum number may be imposed*

Section 19, Housing Act 1961 confers upon a local authority a power which can be exercised in conjunction with, or independently of, a s.15 notice. This is the power to impose a maximum number of individuals or households, or both, who may occupy the house, or any specified part of it, in its present condition. Section 19 can be invoked if the house is in such a state as would justify a s.15 notice, or after s.15 improvements have been made, or in order to forestall a situation which would call for a s.15 notice.

Further, although s.19 occurs in a part of the Act headed 'Houses in Multiple Occupation', and is specifically directed to the purpose of preventing the occurrence of, or remedying, a s.15 situation, it has nevertheless been decided that a local authority can both make and enforce a s.19 direction when the house in question is occupied by a single household only. Moreover, such a direction remains valid on a change of occupation from one family to another, since it is directed to the house rather than its present occupier (*Allen* v. *Khan* [1968] 1 Q.B. 609 (D.C.)).

ii. *When an offence is committed*

It is not an offence that the house, or the particular part of it, continues to be occupied by a number in excess of that set down in the notice. An offence is committed only if the person on whom the notice was served knowingly allows the number in the part of the house to which the notice relates to increase. In addition, if the number decreases, it cannot be supplemented until it falls below the ceiling imposed by the local authority, and it cannot then be increased beyond that ceiling.

iii. *On whom notice may be served*

A s.19 notice may be served on any occupier in respect of his part or, by virtue of s.67(5), Housing Act 1964, on anyone entitled or authorised to permit individuals to take up residence in the house or any part of the house.

iv. *Penalties*

A first offence is punishable by a fine of up to £100, but if the offender has been previously convicted under either s.19, or under s.90 of the 1957 Act, he will be liable to three months' imprisonment in addition to, or instead of, the fine.

c. Power to order improvements to accommodate fewer occupants

Section 67 of the Housing Act 1964 completes the set, and again builds upon the basic provisions of s.15 of the 1961 Act. Section 67 extends the range of a s.15 notice: instead of specifying works necessary to bring a house into suitable condition for its *present* number of occupants, the notice may specify works necessary to render the house suitable for a *smaller* number, and that number may also be adopted by the local authority as the s.19 maximum, should the authority also choose to serve a s.19 notice.

d. Power to impose a management code

Under s.12 of the Housing Act 1961, a local authority may impose a management code upon a house in multiple occupation, if it is of the opinion that the house is in an unsatisfactory condition because of failure to maintain proper standards of management. A copy of the order imposing the code must be served on every owner and lessee, and a copy posted in a prominent position in the house itself.

If thereafter the house becomes defective through failure to comply with the code, or became defective before the code was imposed through failure to meet an equivalent standard of management to that required in the code, the local authority may serve a notice on the manager of the house, requiring him to rectify the condition of the premises (s.14 H.A. 1961). The manager is any owner or lessee who receives payments from tenants or lodgers in the house, or anyone who receives such payments on the owner's or lessee's behalf (s.13 H.A. 1961).

It is a summary offence wilfully to fail to comply with the notice, punishable on first offence by a maximum fine of £100, and on subsequent conviction by a maximum fine of £100, or up to three months' imprisonment, or both (s.65(1) H.A. 1964, and see also s.61 H.A. 1969).

e. Power to require provision of a fire escape

Section 16 of the 1961 Act enables a local authority to direct any person on whom a s.15 notice may be served to provide a multi-occupied house with adequate means of escape from fire, and wilful failure to observe such a direction carries the same penalties as the wilful non-observance of a s.14 or s.15 notice.

5. Local authority duties in relation to overcrowding

These are of a general nature only: it must be stressed that there is no specific or immediate duty upon a local authority to prevent overcrowding, nor any legal responsibility to rehouse any individual or family living in overcrowded conditions, or dispossessed as a consequence of having been overcrowded.

a. Inspection and reporting

The basic general duties are to be found in s.76 of the Housing Act 1957. This obliges a local authority to inspect its district and prepare a report indicating the number of houses needed to overcome the problem of overcrowding in the district, and how these houses are to be provided. The duties only arise, however, if the local authority actually feels that there is occasion to make a report, or if the Minister directs a report to be prepared. In the latter case, the Minister may also fix dates by which 'the said duties' are to be fulfilled. This does not mean that the Minister can direct an authority to abate overcrowding within a particular time; the 'said duties' are only to prepare a scheme for *eventual* abatement.

b. Rehousing

The principal provision with regard to rehousing is contained in s.113(2) of the 1957 Act (see above, pp. 2–3). According to this, the local authority must secure that, in the selection of their tenants, a reasonable preference is given to persons who are occupying overcrowded houses. But since the same preference must also be given to those who are living in accommodation which is unsatisfactory for a variety of other reasons, overcrowding itself is no entitlement to a better home, and the best the individual can hope for is some limited element of preferential consideration.

CHAPTER 6
SQUATTERS

1. The meaning of 'squatter'

'Squatter' is not yet a term of legal art. The word has been used to describe both those who are given temporary permission to occupy premises as a short-term home, and those who take it upon themselves to occupy premises without any prior permission. In law the first group are licensees, the second are trespassers. From this point the word 'squatters' will be used to denote those within the second group only. It was with this second group in mind that Lord Denning M.R. described a squatter as 'one who, without any colour of right, enters on an unoccupied house or land, intending to stay there as long as he can' (*McPhail* v. *Persons Unknown* [1973] Ch. 447 (C.A.)).

2. The civil liability of squatters

Trespass to land is a tort, actionable without proof of damage. The wrong consists in entering on land or premises in the possession of the plaintiff without lawful justification. It is beyond the scope of this book to consider trespass in detail and readers are referred to the standard works.

3. The criminal liability of squatters

Trespass to land is not in itself a criminal offence (hence 'the wooden lie'; trespassers as such cannot be prosecuted). The circumstances which surround a trespass, however, may give rise to criminal liability of several sorts.

a. Forcible entry

The Statute of Forcible Entry 1381 directs that 'none shall henceforth make any entry into any lands and tenements, but in case where entry is given by the law; and in such case not with strong hand, nor with multitude of people, but only in peaceable and easy manner'. Violation of this provision is a criminal offence, punishable by a maximum of two years' imprisonment, or an unlimited fine, or both (Criminal Law Act 1967 s.7(1), (3)).

Although the statute apparently forbids *any* entry, it seems clear that only forcible entries are to be punished (*R.* v. *Smyth* (1832) 5 C. & P. 201), but it is by no means certain what amounts to force for the purposes of the statute. The criterion set down by ABBOTT C.J. in *Milner* v. *Maclean* (1825) 2 C. & P. 17 has been widely invoked. According to this opinion, there must be such a show of force as is calculated to deter the rightful owner from offering resistance or attempting to re-enter.

This seems to suggest that force which is merely directed against the premises in order to gain entry, breaking a lock or smashing a window for instance, is not sufficient to constitute a forcible entry. Nevertheless, the general opinion is that any actual violence, however directed, will suffice (see, e.g. 1971 Criminal Law Review 321–2; Woodfall, *Landlord & Tenant*, 27th Ed. Vol. 1, para. 2247). Certainly the fact that doors or windows have been broken is a relevant circumstance in determining whether force of the *Milner* v. *Maclean* variety was present. So too would be the fact that the squatters entered as a concerted group, whether or not they broke in.

b. Forcible detainer

Forcible detainer is a further criminal offence, and carries the same penalties as forcible entry. The Statute of Forcible Entry 1391 made it a crime to detain by force premises which had been entered by force. Under the Forcible Entry Act of 1429 it is an offence to detain premises by force even if the original entry was peaceable. Hence squatters who enter an unlocked house, or are invited in by those who have gone before, may lay themselves open to prosecution under the 1429 legislation.

The same criterion is used to determine whether a detainer is forcible as is used to decide whether an entry is forcible: was there such a show of force as is calculated to deter the rightful owner from sending the trespasser or trespassers away and resuming his own possession?

What if the squatters barricade themselves in, but make it clear that they will offer no further active resistance to the rightful owner? Since there is then no threat to the rightful owner's person or property it might appear that he would not be deterred from re-entering, but merely inconvenienced by the necessity of having to remove the barricades.

However, in *R.* v. *Robinson (Michael)* [1971] 1 Q.B. 156 the Court of Appeal upheld convictions under the Forcible Entry Act 1429 of defendants who barricaded themselves into premises but offered no further resistance when police eventually reclaimed possession under a High Court order. Although the defendants had conspicuously divested themselves of anything resembling an offensive weapon, it was nevertheless decided that they were guilty of conspiracy to detain by force.

This must not be taken to mean that 'any barricading of a building which caused the true owner to use force in removing the barricades necessarily amounted to the use of force in retention'. Although the matter is not made clear in *Robinson*, one may surmise that force is present only if the true owner is led, by all the circumstances, to expect active resistance. Erecting heavy barricades is an indication that the occupants intend such resistance, particularly if they are there in numbers, and divesting oneself of weapons does not exclude the possibility of active, and violent, opposition.

Although the Forcible Entry Act 1429 gives summary jurisdiction to justices of the peace, both forcible entry and forcible detainer are triable on indictment, and this is in fact the usual method of prosecution (*R.* v. *Mountford* [1972] Q.B. 28 (C.A.)).

c. Criminal Damage

'A person who without lawful excuse destroys or damages any property belonging to another intending to destroy or damage any such property or being reckless as to whether any such property would be destroyed or damaged is guilty of an offence' (s.1, Criminal Damage Act 1971).

This offence, if tried on indictment, carries a maximum penalty of ten years' imprisonment (s.4(2)). The offence is triable summarily with the consent of the accused, but the accused has no *right* to summary trial.

Squatters who smash locks or windows in order to enter premises expose themselves to prosecution under this Act. They will also be liable if the premises, once occupied, are damaged in any way, as, for example, by writing on the walls or causing the drains to block, provided the requisite mental element of the crime is present (see J. C. Smith & B. Hogan, *Criminal Law*, 3rd Edn, Butterworths, Ch. 17).

d. Conspiracy to trespass

A criminal conspiracy is an agreement between two or more persons to carry out some unlawful purpose, and it is a common law offence punishable at the discretion of the court. The offence is complete once the agreement is made; there is no requirement that the conspirators implement their common intention, or carry it to a successful conclusion.

What constitutes an unlawful purpose, so as to render an agreement to effect that purpose a criminal conspiracy? Clearly a crime is an unlawful purpose; thus it is a criminal conspiracy for two or more intending squatters to agree to commit any of the above offences (see, e.g. *R.* v. *Robinson* (above, p. 82), and *per* LORD HAILSHAM L.C. in *Kamara* v. *D.P.P.* [1974] A.C. 104 at p. 126C (H.L.)).

The circumstances in which an agreement to commit the tort of trespass can constitute the crime of conspiracy were considered by the House of Lords in *Kamara* v. *D.P.P.* A group of students had occupied the Sierra Leone High

Commission as a gesture of opposition to the ruling regime, and they were indicted with conspiracy to trespass. It was argued on the defendants' behalf that no such offence was known to the law or, alternatively, that a tort is an unlawful purpose only if accompanied by malice or fraud.

These contentions were rejected, but the House of Lords did not adopt the extreme view which had been taken by the Court of Appeal in the same case, that an agreement to commit a tort is, without more, an indictable conspiracy. According to LORD HAILSHAM L.C., an agreement to trespass will be indictable as a conspiracy if the objective of the agreement is either 'the invasion of the public domain', or the infliction of 'injury and damage which goes beyond the field of the nominal'. Such injury and damage is inflicted 'where the intention is to occupy premises to the exclusion of the owner's right, either by expelling him altogether or otherwise effectively preventing him from enjoying his property'.

It appears to follow from this that squatters who plan their action together thereby commit the offence of conspiracy, if they intend, as is usually the case, to deprive the rightful owner of his property, albeit for a limited time and by peaceable means (see Law Commission Working Paper no. 54, para. 28).

An honest belief in *facts* which would render the purpose legal is a good defence, however. Thus it would be a defence for the conspirators to show that they thought permission to occupy the premises had been given by the owner. It would be no defence to show a belief that the owner would not object if asked, as this is speculation, not fact. Nor would it be a defence if squatters mistakenly believed that their urgent need for shelter and housing justified an otherwise unlawful action, since necessity is no defence to a crime arising out of squatting, and the mistake is one of law.

e. Law Commission proposals

The existing law is based upon medieval legislation of uncertain scope and obscure terminology. The Law Commission, believing this uncertainty is conductive to public disorder, has proposed, in its Working Paper no. 54, that the offences of forcible entry, forcible detainer, and conspiracy to trespass should be abolished. In their place two new offences would arise:

(*a*) Without lawful authority entering property by force adversely to any person in physical occupation of it, or entitled to occupy it; and

(*b*) being unlawfully on property and failing to leave as soon as reasonably practicable after being ordered to leave by a person entitled to occupation.

'Force' would be redefined in terms restricting it to behaviour likely to dissuade a person of reasonable fortitude, for fear of violence to his person, from offering lawful resistance. Fear for one's property would, presumably, no longer be sufficient.

The first proposed offence would carry a maximum penalty of two years' imprisonment, and the second a maximum of six months.

4. Eviction of squatters

a. Without a court order

If a person who is entitled to possession of premises currently occupied by a squatter forcibly removes him, without first obtaining an order for possession from the County court or High Court, does that person incur any civil or criminal liability as a result?

i. *Civil liability*

The common law rule is that no civil liability is incurred towards a trespasser by forcibly ejecting him, provided that no more force is used than is reasonably necessary in the circumstances. In many situations this rule simply reflects the common sense of the matter. No one would expect a householder to obtain a possession order before removing a tramp found sleeping in the garage, or deny a farmer the right to expel campers who had pitched a tent in his field without permission, though such acts might be considered ungenerous or uncharitable.

A squatter presents a somewhat different problem. He is someone who has established himself in premises, intending to make them his home, to the exclusion of the rightful owner. Almost invariably the premises were previously unoccupied. The squatter may have moved in furniture, or done repair work to make the premises habitable. He may be there in a group, whose removal might necessitate the use of considerable force. Is the owner to be allowed to resort to self-help, and is the squatter to be denied the protection of the rule that only reasonable force may be used against him?

In *Hemmings* v. *Stoke Poges Golf Club* [1920] 1. K.B. 720, the Court of Appeal decided that the common law rule is unaffected by the Statutes of Forcible Entry, regardless of whether the forcible eviction of a trespasser is a criminal offence under the Act of 1381. An ex-employee and his wife sought to recover damages under the Statute of Forcible Entry 1381, for trespass, assault and battery, from the husband's former employers. During the period of employment the plaintiffs had occupied a cottage, owned by the defendants, under a service licence. After the employment ended the plaintiffs were given valid notice to quit the cottage, but refused to leave. Upon expiry of the notice they became trespassers, and the defendants eventually removed them, using no more force than was reasonably necessary in the circumstances (n.b. now, however, s.32 R.A. 1965, below pp. 100–2).

The plaintiffs claimed that the Statute of Forcible Entry 1381 imposed civil as well as criminal liability. This contention was rejected by the Court of Appeal. Even if the defendants had violated the 1381 Act (which was not in issue and not decided) no civil liability was incurred thereby. SCRUTTON L.J. entered this important caveat, however:

> It will remain the law that a person who replies to a

> claim for trespass and assault that he ejected a trespasser on his property with no more force than was necessary may be successfully met by the reply that he used more force than was necessary . . . The risk of paying damages and costs on this finding and the danger of becoming liable to prosecution under the Statutes of Forcible Entry may well deter people from exercising this remedy except by order of the court.

In view of these risks, an owner or other claimant would often be well advised to obtain a court order for possession, rather than taking the law into his own hands.

ii. *Criminal liability*

But is the person who ejects a trespasser with force in fact criminally liable under the Act of 1381? It has been suggested that no such liability is incurred. In the *Hemmings* case, DUKE L.J., having noted that authority is divided upon the question of whether a prosecution for forcible entry can be brought for the forcible eviction of a trespasser, concluded that the more recent decisions recognise such liability, provided that the trespasser has been forcibly removed from *possession.* In *McPhail* v. *Persons Unknown* (above, p. 80), LORD DENNING M.R. declaimed that trespassers cannot gain possession of premises, in the strict legal sense, without the acquiescence of the owner. Therefore no offence is committed under the 1381 Act by removing the trespassers without a court order, at least where the owner acts quickly. (If he delays, he may be deemed to have acquiesced in the occupation.) The case is presumably different where the occupant becomes a trespasser only by virtue of permission to occupy being withdrawn or coming to an end. Here there has been possession, which will continue, albeit as adverse possession, after the occupant's change of status from licensee or tenant to trespasser.

Lord Denning's opinion has been strongly criticised (see, e.g. (1973) 89 L.Q.R. 458; 1973 C.L.J. 220; L.A.G. Bull.

January 1975 11, 14). The Law Commission, in its Working Paper no. 54, described it as oversimplified. Nevertheless, it remains difficult to determine when, and in what circumstances, a trespasser will gain the possession necessary to draw him within the aegis of the Statute of Forcible Entry.

Section 30 of the Rent Act 1965 makes it a criminal offence to harass or unlawfully evict the residential occupier of any premises (below, pp. 140–4). Squatters who have occupied premises as their home will satisfy the definition of residential occupiers, and so be protected by these provisions, only if it can be said that the right of any other person to recover possession of the premises is restricted by some enactment or rule of law (see s.30(5) R.A. 1965). It seems that these provisions do not extend the protection of the criminal law beyond the categories of residents already protected by the forcible entry legislation. If it were once established that squatters may be within these Acts, however, they would then also satisfy the definition of residential occupiers for the purposes of s.30 R.A. 1965.

b. With a court order

i. *By originating summons*

A new and speedy procedure for the recovery of land or premises occupied by trespassers is provided by Order 113 of the Rules of the Supreme Court (for actions in the High Court) and Order 26 of the County Court Rules (for actions in the County court). County court jurisdiction in this respect is limited to actions for the recovery of land or premises with a net annual value for rating of not more than £1,000.

These orders were introduced in 1971 to overcome deficiencies in the previous procedure revealed in *Manchester Corporation* v. *Connolly* [1970] 1 Ch. 420 (C.A.) and *In re Wykeham Terrace, Brighton, Sussex, ex parte T.A.V.R.A.* [1971] 1 Ch. 204. The former case revealed that an order for possession could not be made on an interlocutory application, but only as a final judgment; the latter showed that squatters could defeat the old procedure altogether by refusing to give their names, or squatting in shifts, since that procedure was only available against a named defendant or defendants.

Order 113 provides as follows (Order 26 is in substantially the same terms):

> Where a person claims possession of land which he alleges is occupied solely by a person or persons (not being a tenant or tenants holding over after the termination of the tenancy) who entered into or remained in occupation without his licence or consent or that of any predecessor in title of his, the proceedings may be brought by originating summons in accordance with the provisions of this Order.

Order 113 and Order 26 can be invoked only in cases where there is no arguable defence, and no other claim (e.g. for damages) can be joined to the claim for possession in these proceedings.

ii. *Form of summons and affidavit*

The originating summons must be in one of two specified forms; Form 10 must be used where all the occupants of the land or premises have been identified and Form 11A where the claimant has been unable, after taking reasonable steps, to identify every person occupying the land or premises for the purpose of making him a defendant.

A summons will be dismissed if the claimant has not taken reasonable steps to identify all the occupants: 'this very special procedure enabling a person claiming possession to proceed on a summons not naming the alleged occupant must be strictly complied with' according to PENNYCUICK V-C in *Re Orpen Road (No. 9), Stoke Newington* [1971] 1 All E.R.944.

Whichever form is used, the claimant must file an affidavit in support of the summons, setting out his interest in the land, and the circumstances in which it has been occupied without licence or consent and in which his claim to possession arises. In addition, if Form 11A is used, the affidavit must state that the claimant has taken all reasonable steps to identify the occupants, and describe the steps actually taken.

iii. *Service*

The summons and a copy of the affidavit must be served on every named defendant. Where there are unnamed defendants a copy of the summons must be affixed to some conspicuous part of the premises, such as the front door.

iv. *Possession order*

Normally, a final order for possession will not be made until at least seven clear days have elapsed from the date on which the summons was served. The court may, however, make an order within that period in a case of urgency. In *Mercy* v. *Persons Unknown, The Times* 5th June 1974 (C.A.) squatters occupied a house which was in the process of being converted into flats. The owner feared that the newly decorated flats would be ruined, and become less attractive to prospective tenants. The Court of Appeal declined to regard the case as urgent on these facts. Residents returning from holiday to find their house taken over by squatters might present a suitable case of urgency.

The Court of Appeal has also ruled, in *McPhail* v. *Persons Unknown* (above, p. 80), that a judge has no power to delay enforcement of a possession order (see also *Department of the Environment* v. *James* [1972] 1 W.L.R. 1279). The reason for this supposed lack of jurisdiction is said to lie in the fact that an owner can retake premises from squatters without need of a court order. So, if the owner chooses to come to court first, he should not be in a worse position than if he had resorted to self-help. The logic of this is incontrovertible, once one accepts the initial premise. However, despite *McPhail's* case, it is still open to question whether squatters can in fact be removed with impunity without the prior sanction of the court.

It is no defence to a claim for possession made by a local authority under Order 113 that the defendants occupied local authority premises as a matter of necessity, after the local authority had wrongly failed to provide the defendants with temporary emergency accommodation under s.21(1)(*b*) of the National Assistance Act 1948 (*Southwark L.B.C.* v. *Williams* [1971] Ch. 734 (C.A.)).

CHAPTER 7

LICENCES

See generally L.A.G. Bull. July 1974, p. 155.

1. Distinction between a licence and a tenancy

a. Generally

A person who is occupying premises with the consent of someone with an estate or interest in those premises may be occupying them under a licence or a tenancy. A licence is simply a permission to occupy premises, but a tenancy is an estate or interest in the premises themselves.

However, these familiar descriptions do not provide the means for determining, in any particular case, whether a tenancy or a licence has been granted. There is no single definition or criterion which will serve to distinguish a licensee from a tenant: each case depends upon its own particular circumstances. In many cases, where the facts are blurred or the parties have behaved in an ambivalent fashion, it will be a nice question whether the relationship which has been created is that of landlord and tenant, or licensor and licensee. In many other cases, however, it will be obvious.

Furthermore, there are different types of licences, with different legal incidents attached to each type. It is therefore necessary, first of all, to decide whether or not premises are occupied under a licence, and, if they are, to identify the type of licence involved.

It is usually said to be a matter of the parties' intention whether there is a licence or a tenancy in a particular case, and that no single factor is conclusive. Questions of intention are notoriously difficult to resolve, however, and, at the end of the day, are often settled by the court weighing all relevant factors for and against a particular conclusion in a common-sense manner. Thus the result of each case will depend upon the balance of its own individual circumstances.

b. The name given to the relationship

Certain general observations can be made, however. First of all, the name which the parties may happen to give their relationship will not decide the matter: simply calling an agreement to occupy premises a licence (or a tenancy) will not make it one, if the balance of factors points to its being something else (see, e.g. *Errington* v. *Errington & Woods* [1952] 1 K.B. 290 at 298 (C.A.)). It does not even raise a presumption that the relationship is in fact as the parties have described it. Thus, even if the parties are aware of the legal significance of the distinction and wish, say, to avoid the incidents of a tenancy agreement, this will not be achieved merely by attaching a particular label. (It is not unknown for landlords, when letting premises, to attempt to deprive the tenant of his statutory security of tenure, or to escape statutory repairing obligations, by describing the occupancy as being under a licence. This device is legally unsound, though it may in practice achieve its object against an ignorant tenant (see the Report of the Committee on Housing in Greater London (the Holland Report) 1965 Cmnd 2605 pp. 171, 2; the Report on the Rent Acts (the Francis Report) 1971 Cmnd 4609 and L.A.G. Bull. July 1974 p. 162).

c. Exclusive possession

Second, although it is a prerequisite of a tenancy that the tenant be given exclusive possession of the premises, in the sense of a general right to exclude all others, including the landlord, the granting of exclusive possession is no longer sufficient in itself to identify a tenancy, (although this was once thought to be so: see, e.g. *Lynes* v. *Snaith* [1899] 1 Q.B. 486). It is now uncertain how much weight must be given to exclusive possession. In *Addiscombe Garden Estates Ltd* v.

Crabbe [1958] 1 Q.B. 513 (C.A.) JENKINS L.J. called it a consideration of the first importance, but, more recently, SACHS L.J. has suggested that exclusive possession is a factor which 'appears nowadays to have diminishing weight' (*Barnes* v. *Barratt* [1970] 2 Q.B. 657 (C.A.)).

The granting of exclusive possession will, however, raise a presumption in favour of a tenancy, though this may be displaced by a preponderance of other circumstances indicating an intention merely to give a licence to occupy (*Errington* v. *Errington & Woods* above, p. 93; *Heslop* v. *Burns* [1974] 3 All E.R. 406 (C.A.)).

d. Other factors

Other factors which point towards the conclusion that a tenancy, and not a licence, has been granted include the following:

(*a*) An express repairing obligation placed upon the prospective occupier; 'It seems inappropriate that a mere licensee should be saddled with an obligation to repair': *per* JENKINS L.J. in the *Addiscombe Garden Estates* case.

(*b*) Reservation by the grantor of an express right to enter and inspect the premises. In the absence of an express reservation a *landlord* has no right to enter the demised premises. The express reservation of such a right therefore suggests that the parties had a tenancy and not a licence in mind.

(*c*) An express covenant of quiet enjoyment, or an express right to determine on non-payment of rent. Once again, these are terms in an agreement which are typical of a tenancy rather than a licence.

Finally, in *Facchini* v. *Bryson* [1952] 1 T.L.R. 1386 (C.A.) DENNING L.J. commented that 'in all cases where an occupier has been held to be a licensee there has been something in the circumstances, such as a family arrangement, an act of friendship or generosity, or such like, to negative any intention to create a tenancy. In such circumstances it would be obviously unjust to saddle the owner with a tenancy, with all the momentous consequences that that entails nowadays. . . .'

This, therefore, is a factor which will weigh on the side of a licence and against a lease, although in some cases it may negative any intention to create legal relations at all (*Heslop* v. *Burns*, above, p. 94).

2. The types of licence

a. The gratuitous licence

i. *Definition*

A gratuitous licensee is someone who is allowed to use or occupy premises but gives nothing in return. The weekend guest, the campers whom a farmer allows to pitch a tent or bring a caravan on his land without payment and the homeless family given a night's shelter all fall within this category, as well as those who are allowed to reside for longer periods without making any payment.

ii. *Revocation*

Generally speaking, the gratuitous licensee is entitled to a reasonable amount of notice before he can be made to leave. The licensor may specify a particular shorter period, however, when granting the licence. The notice may be implicit in the nature of the licence, or in the circumstances in which the licence is asked for or granted. An invitation to stay for the weekend or a request for a night's shelter contain their own limitations, and no further, more formal, notice is required to terminate such licences.

Apart from this, it is a question of fact as to what constitutes a reasonable amount of notice. For instance, the time it will take the licensee to find alternative accommodation may be relevant. At the least, a licensee is entitled to enough time to collect his possessions together and remove them from the premises. Even if insufficient time is allowed, however, the notice of revocation itself will be valid, so that the licensee must still leave after a reasonable time (*Minister of Health* v. *Belotti* [1944] K.B. 298).

iii. *Recovery of possession*

After the notice expires the licensee who stays on without further permission becomes a trespasser, and is amenable to the summary procedure for recovery of possession laid down in Order 113 R.S.C. and Order 26 C.C.R. (above, pp. 88–91). This procedure can in fact be utilised against *all* erstwhile licensees. The gratuitous licensee is in all probability protected from forcible removal, however, under the Forcible Entry Acts, by virtue of his previous possession (above, pp. 87–8).

b. The contractual residential licence

i. *Under Part VI, Rent Act 1968*

In *Luganda* v. *Service Hotels Ltd* [1969] 2 All E.R. 692 (C.A.) the Court of Appeal acknowledged that licensees who satisfy certain conditions are entitled to the protection of Part VI of the Rent Act 1968. This gives occupants under a so-called Part VI contract a right of access to a rent tribunal for consideration of the rent payable under the contract, and allows the tribunal to grant a limited security of tenure, provided in this latter case that the contract was not for a fixed term. (This is because the security takes the form of a suspension of the notice to quit, and if the contract is for a fixed term no notice to quit need be served, since the right of occupation will terminate automatically at the end of the term).

Part VI applies to a contract under which one person grants to another the right to occupy as a residence a dwelling to which Part VI applies, in consideration of a rent which includes some payment for the use of furniture or for services (s.70(1) R.A. 1968).

The dwellings to which Part VI applies are those of or

below a specified rateable value on the so-called appropriate day. The appropriate day is defined in s.6 as 23rd March 1965 for a dwelling which, on that date, was or was part of premises for which a rateable value was shown in the valuation list then in force. For a dwelling which was not rated on 23rd March 1965, the appropriate day is the date on which a rateable value was first shown in the valuation list.

Where the appropriate day falls *before* 1st April 1973, the rateable value ceilings for Part VI are £400 for a dwelling in Greater London, and £200 for a dwelling elsewhere. However, a dwelling which falls outside the relevant figure on the appropriate day will still be subject to Part VI if its rateable value on 1st April 1973 did not exceed £1,500 in Greater London or £750 elsewhere.

Where the appropriate day comes on or after 1st April 1973, the ceiling is £1,500 for a dwelling in Greater London, and £750 for a dwelling elsewhere.

For the purposes of Part VI, a dwelling can be part of a house as well as the whole. If the contract relates to part only, an appropriate proportion of the total rateable value is taken, so that, although the house as a whole might be outside the rent tribunal's jurisdiction, the particular part may fall within it (ss.6(1)(*b*), 81 R.A. 1968). Furthermore, it has been decided that, for the purposes of Part VI, a 'house' signifies a building in which people live, whether or not it was originally built as a dwelling (*per* LORD DENNING M.R. in *Luganda* at p. 694).

In *Luganda*'s case the defendants operated a residential hotel, in which each of the eighty-eight rooms was fitted out as a bed-sitter. The defendants provided a gas-ring, some furniture, bedding, and various services. The plaintiff, who had occupied one such room for almost three years, objected to an increase in his rent, and applied for advice to the local rent tribunal. The defendants, when they learned of this, gave him notice to quit and, after this notice had expired, barred him from his room, which they quickly re-let.

The plaintiff sought an interlocutory injunction to restore his access and to prevent the defendants from interfering further. The court decided that he was within the protection of Part VI, even though he was only a contractual licensee and not a tenant, and therefore entitled to the order sought.

From this case and from Part VI itself it emerges that a contractual licensee will be entitled to protection from a rent tribunal if the following conditions are satisfied:

(*a*) the licensee must have exclusive occupation of some part of the premises, whether or not he also shares other accommodation, such as a bathroom or kitchen (s.70(2) R.A. 1968). Exclusive occupation of a single room suffices (*Thurrock U.D.C.* v. *Shina* (1972) 23 P. & C.R. 205 (D.C.)). Exclusive occupation is not the same as exclusive possession, in the sense of a right to exclude the landlord and all others from the premises: 'A person has a right to exclusive occupation of a room when he is entitled to occupy it himself, and no one else is entitled to occupy it', according to LORD DENNING M.R. in *Luganda*. It is both necessary and sufficient, according to this view, that the licensee has the right to prevent anyone else from *living* in the room or rooms, even though the licensor may have extensive rights of access (*R.* v. *Battersea etc Rent Tribunal, ex parte Parikh* [1957] 1 All E.R. 352 (C.A.)). If he can be required to share all the rooms, however, he is not protected by Part VI. Similarly, joint licensees must be able to prevent anyone else from being given a right to occupy the rooms in the future (see L.A.G. Bull. July 1974 p. 163).

(*b*) The licensee must have the right to occupy the premises *as a residence*. Whereas statutory tenants lose the protection of Part II of the Rent Act 1968 (below, p. 118) if they actually cease to reside in the premises, Part VI of the Act does not require that the right of occupation actually be exercised. The right to occupy as a residence can be implied, and need not be spelled out in the contract (*R.* v. *York etc Rent Tribunal, ex parte Ingle* [1954] 1 Q.B. 456 (D.C.)).

This requirement excludes the normal hotel guest from protection, even if he has been staying for a considerable time, unless a residential licence can be implied from other circumstances. In addition, s.70(5) R.A. 1968 provides that no right to occupy a dwelling for a holiday is to be treated for the purposes of Part VI as a right to occupy it as a residence.

(*c*) The licensee must pay rent, that is, he must supply a monetary consideration. Thus the person who is given a room in return for services—e.g. a tramp who is allowed to sleep in the garage in return for digging the garden—is not protected by Part VI, even if he satisfies the other requirements, unless the value of the service can be quantified (*Barnes* v. *Barratt* [1970] 2 Q.B. 657 (C.A.)).

(*d*) Furthermore, that rent must include some payment for the use of furniture or services (s.70(1) R.A. 1968). Subject to the *de minimis* rule, it does not matter that the amount of rent attributable to furniture or services is slight.

Services are defined in s.84(1) R.A. 1968 to include attendance, the provision of heating or lighting, the supply of hot water, and any other privilege or facility connected with the occupancy of a dwelling, other than a privilege or facility requisite for the purposes of access, cold water supply, or sanitary accommodation.

If light, heating, and hot water are paid for by the licensee into a slot-meter, or direct to the undertaker, he will not come within this provision. Nor will the licensee be protected if he is supplied with the service only in a part of the house which he shares with others, e.g. clean towels or hot water in a communal bathroom.

(*e*) The rent must *not* include any payment in respect of board, if the value of that board to the lessee forms a substantial proportion of the whole rent (s.70(3)(*b*) R.A. 1968).

Board connotes the provision of a meal or meals: a morning cup of tea or an evening mug of cocoa is not board (*per* YOUNGER L.J. in *Wilkes* v. *Goodwin* [1923] 2 K.B. 86 at 110 (C.A.)). The value of the board must be substantial *to the tenant*, so the licensor will not escape Part VI merely by attributing a large part of the rent to the provision of what is in fact insubstantial board.

(*f*) As has already been seen, the licence must be periodic in order for a rent tribunal to be able to grant any extension of tenure.

(*g*) Although premises which are let by a local authority cannot be the subject of a protected tenancy under Part II, there is no equivalent limitation regarding Part VI contracts. However, s.158(1) H.A. 1957 (as amended) provides that nothing in the Rent Act 1968 shall prevent a local authority from recovering possession of any house if it is required to enable the authority to exercise any of its statutory housing powers. It is sufficient in this respect for the local authority to show that the dwelling is required for another occupant (*St Pancras B.C.* v. *Frey* [1963] 2 All E.R. 124 (D.C.), but see also L.A.G. Bull. Sept. 1973 pp. 198–9).

ii. *Service licences*

A service licensee is someone who is given a residential licence in connection with or in consequence of his particular employment. This sort of licence is also called a service occupancy. A service licensee will come within the *Luganda* principle if he satisfies the conditions outlined above. Whether or not he does this, however, the service licensee is given specific statutory protection, albeit of a very limited kind, by s.32 of the Rent Act 1965.

Section 32(1) provides that, where any premises have been let as a dwelling which is not a protected tenancy (below, pp. 108–16) and that tenancy has come to an end, but the occupier continues to reside in the premises or a part of them, it shall not be lawful for the owner to enforce his right to recover possession of the premises, except by proceedings in court.

By virtue of subsection (2), this protection extends to an occupier who was not a tenant, but was given exclusive possession of any premises under the terms of his employment.

It should be noted, first of all, that, unlike Part VI of the 1968 Act, s.32(2) requires that the service licensee have exclusive *possession.* Since it is also likely that the element of favour mentioned by DENNING L.J. in *Facchini* v. *Bryson* (above, p. 94) will not be present, there must be a predominance of other factors to suggest that occupation is under a licence rather than a service tenancy. One such case in which these factors were present is *Warder* v. *Cooper* [1970] 1 Ch. 495, which also illustrates the extent of protection given to an erstwhile service licensee by s.32(2).

The defendant ran a garage and service station on land which he rented for the purpose. A bungalow stood on the land, which was available, under the terms of the lease, for employees of the garage. A service licence only could be granted, however; the defendant could not *sublet* the bungalow, The plaintiff was engaged as foreman, the employment to be determinable by two weeks' notice, and the bungalow was provided for the plaintiff rent-free.

After a few weeks the plaintiff was given notice terminating his employment. After the notice had expired, and while the plaintiff was away for a weekend, the defendant changed the locks on the bungalow. The plaintiff sought and was granted an interim injunction to restrain the defendant from interfering with his access to and use of the bungalow.

STAMP J. decided that the plaintiff had not established that he was, prima facie, a tenant. Three factors pointed to his being a licensee only: no rent was specified to be payable under his agreement with the defendant; the landlord could not sublet the bungalow without breaking his own covenant in the lease; and the plaintiff's employment was liable to be determined on very short notice.

Nevertheless, the plaintiff was entitled to the injunction which he sought, since s.32 R.A. 1965 was meant to protect that very class of persons of which the plaintiff was one, and to prevent their eviction otherwise than by the order of a court.

According to STAMP J. in this case, violation of s.32 is actionable as a tort. It will also involve the offence of unlawful eviction under s.30(1) of the 1965 Act (see below, pp. 144–5).

The licensee will lose the protection of s.32 if, after termination of the licence, he ceases to reside in at least a part of the premises. Whether or not he has given up residence is a question of fact: a mere temporary absence will not deprive him of protection, especially if he retains some symbol of his continued residence, such as furniture, on the premises (see further below, p. 118).

iii. *Other contractual residential licences*

This residual category covers a wide range of licensees, including service licensees who have not been given exclusive possession and are not protected by Part VI; and non-service licensees who supply an unquantifiable non-monetary consideration, or who receive substantial board, or who are given neither furniture nor services, or who occupy premises without a right of residence (e.g. holiday licensees or guests in a non-residential hotel) or who do not have exclusive occupation.

These licensees enjoy the same basic protection which the law affords to gratuitous licensees, but, beyond this, they must look to the general law of contract.

3. Revocation of a contractual licence

a. Where the licence is validly revoked

A contractual licence is validly revoked when the proper period of notice has been given and elapsed, or when the period for which the licence was given has expired. One who holds over beyond this period is a trespasser. While it is almost certain that his forcible removal without a court order would violate the Statute of Forcible Entry 1381, and thereby s.30(1) of the Rent Act 1965, the speedy procedure for recovery of possession introduced by Order 113 R.S.C. and Order 26 C.C.R. (above, pp. 88–91) is available against former licensees as well as against those who were trespassers from the very outset (*Bristol Corporation* v. *Persons Unknown* [1974] 1 All E.R. 593).

Those who were long-term residential licensees are equally amenable to this procedure, provided that the licence has been properly terminated. Contrary to the note to Order 113 in the Supreme Court Practice (1973) 1481 and to the opinion of Pennycuick v–c in the *Britsol Corporation* case (above), a court has no discretion as to the type of licence which is subject to Order 113 or Order 26 (*G.L.C.* v. *Jenkins* [1975] 1 All E.R. 354 (C.A.)).

However, although Pennycuick v-c felt constrained to grant an order for immediate possession against the former licensees in the *Bristol Corporation* case, it has been strongly urged that it *is* within the discretion of a court to suspend the operation of a possession order against a former licensee since (unlike squatters) former licensees who hold over do have possession, and so cannot be forcibly evicted without the sanction of a court. Hence the much-criticised argument invoked by Lord Denning m.r. in *McPhail* v. *Persons Unknown* (above, p. 80) based upon a squatter's supposed lack of possession, is inapplicable to former licensees (see also L.A.G. Bull. July 1974 p. 160).

b. Where the licence is invalidly revoked

A licensee is, not unnaturally, in a much stronger position if his licence has been wrongfully revoked, although this has not always been the case. It was established in the courts of common law, before the fusion of law and equity by the Judicature Acts 1873–5, that the wrongful revocation of a contractual licence, even though it amounted to a breach entitling the licensee to damages, was nevertheless effective to terminate the licence. After a reasonable time the licensee became a trespasser, and could be forcibly removed without the licensor incurring any tortious liability thereby, provided that no more than reasonable force was used (*Wood* v. *Leadbitter* (1845) 13 M. & W. 838; *Kerrison* v. *Smith* [1897] 2 Q.B. 445).

The attitude of equity now prevails: in an appropriate case a court will grant an equitable remedy—specific performance or an injunction—to ensure that the primary obligations of a contractual licence are observed (see generally *Winter Garden Theatre (London) Ltd* v. *Millennium Productions Ltd* [1948] A.C. 173 (H.L.)).

Such a remedy is unlikely to be granted where the licensor and licensee share the same premises, except, perhaps, if each occupies a completely separate part, with a separate access (*Thompson* v. *Park* [1944] K.B. 408 (C.A.)).

The forcible removal of a contractual licensee during the currency of his licence is a tort (*Hurst* v. *Picture Theatres Ltd* [1915] 1 K.B. 1 (C.A.)).

4. The contractual licence and third parties

The question whether a contractual licence binds third parties is controversial. The classic definition of a licence (see e.g. *Thomas* v. *Sorrell* (1673) Vaugh. 330) makes plain that a licence merely signifies a personal relationship between licensor and licensee, whereas a lease is property, an interest in the land itself. This dichotomy is reinforced by the doctrine of privity of contract, according to which purely personal contractual rights can arise only between the contracting parties themselves. Third parties, outsiders to the contract, are not bound by the agreement.

This clear conceptual line between a licence and a lease has faded and shifted since the time it was first drawn. It has been recognised, at least by some judges, that a contractual licence may bind third parties in certain circumstances. It is difficult, however, to state with certainty the extent to which (or, indeed, the reason why) a purely contractual licence to occupy premises or land will bind the successors in title to the original licensor.

The strongest support for the view that contractual licences are binding against third parties is to be found in the judgment of DENNING L.J. in *Errington* v. *Errington & Woods* (above, p. 93), in which he asserted that 'contractual licences now have a force and validity of their own and cannot be revoked in breach of the contract. Neither the licensor nor anyone who claims through him can disregard the contract except a purchaser for value without notice'.

This opinion, which obfuscates the distinction between real and personal rights, has engendered considerable opposition (see, e.g. *National Provincial Bank Ltd* v. *Hastings Car Mart Ltd* [1965] A.C. 1175 (H.L.); *In re Solomon, a Bankrupt* [1967] 1 Ch. 573, and Wade 68 L.Q.R. 337). Thus, while it is well established that a licence coupled with an interest in the land to which the licence relates (e.g. a right to come on to land and take wood, or a right to a conveyance of the land after the licensee has paid off a mortgage) binds third parties, judicial opinion at present does not, in general, appear to favour the transformation of a purely contractual licence into something which is effectively a new interest in land.

It is possible, however, that third parties who acquire licensed land or premises with knowledge of the licence may be bound by it for other reasons than that put forward in *Errington* v. *Errington & Woods*. First of all, if third parties acquire the land or premises *expressly subject* to the licence, they may be held to be under a constructive trust in favour of the licensee (*Binions* v. *Evans* [1972] Ch. 359 (C.A.), but cf. generally *Re Schebsman* [1944] Ch. 83 (C.A.)).

Alternatively, it has been suggested that third parties who acquire land with knowledge of a licence and then evict the contractual licensee are guilty of the tort of interference with existing contractual rights. A court could then intervene, by way of injunction, to restrain that interference (*per* MEGAW L.J. in *Binions* v. *Evans* at p. 371).

CHAPTER 8

SECURITY OF TENURE

The extent to which a residential *tenant*, as opposed to a mere *licensee*, is secure against eviction depends upon the category into which the particular tenancy falls. There are three such categories, for these purposes: tenancies within Part II of the Rent Act 1968, as amended; those within Part VI of the same Act, as amended; and those whose only source of protection is Part III of the Rent Act 1965.

1. Security of tenure under Part II, Rent Act 1968

These tenancies benefit from the highest degree of security which the law allows. The tenant cannot, moreover, be deprived of this security by agreement with his landlord. Part II does, however, apply to tenancies only, and does not, like Part VI, extend to contractual licences.

a. Terminology

Tenancies within Part II are described by four different terms: protected, statutory, regulated, and controlled. The first two terms are mutually exclusive, as are the second two: i.e. a protected tenancy is *either* regulated *or* controlled, and a statutory tenancy is *either* regulated *or* controlled.

A protected tenancy is defined in s.1 of the 1968 Act. The phrase is applicable only during the contractual currency of the lease or agreement. Once the contractual period ends, either after the expiry of a valid notice to quit (where the tenancy is periodic) or automatically at the end of the fixed term, the protected tenant becomes a statutory tenant (s.3 R.A. 1968).

A statutory tenancy is not, properly speaking, a tenancy at

all. The phrase describes a personal right of the formerly protected tenant to remain in residential occupation after the contractual period. This right can pass to others only in certain limited circumstances (below, p. 119). A statutory tenancy can only follow a protected tenancy.

The protected tenancy, and the statutory tenancy which follows it, are either regulated or controlled. This distinction is drawn according to factors set out in Schedule 2, Part I, and its chief importance is that different sets of provisions as to rent apply to regulated and controlled tenancies; there are also some differences in the security of tenure which each type of tenant enjoys.

A regulated tenancy is defined in the Rent Act 1968 in negative terms as a protected or statutory tenancy which is not (because it never was or because it has ceased to be) a controlled tenancy (s.7(2)). The phrase in parenthesis indicates that there is a statutory mechanism for converting controlled tenancies into regulated tenancies with the ultimate objective of subjecting all protected or statutory tenancies to the same regime of rent restriction. This process, and its implications, are beyond the scope of this book (see T. M. Aldridge, *Rent Control and Leasehold Enfranchisement*, 6th Edn, Oyez Publishing Limited). Generally speaking, so far as Part II security of tenure is concerned, it is sufficient that the tenancy is protected or statutory, whether as a regulated or as a controlled tenancy.

b. Protected tenancies

Residential tenancies are protected if the following conditions are satisfied:

i. *The tenancy must be of a dwelling-house*

The tenancy must relate to a dwelling-house which must be let to the tenant as a separate dwelling (s.1 R.A. 1968).

The house may, in fact, be part of a larger structure, but apart from this, 'dwelling-house' is not defined in the 1968 Act. One may assume, however, that the term comprehends any structure in which people make their home (cf. *Stott* v.

Hefferon [1974] 3 All E.R. 673 (D.C.) where, for the purposes of s.90 of the National Insurance Act 1965, a dwelling-house is somewhere where people dwell, and not merely a place originally built as a dwelling). In *Spraggs* v. *Prentice* (1950) 100 L.J. 541 (County court) a three-roomed beach hut was held to be a dwelling-house, though not a permanent building, because it was fitted out in such a way that the occupants could use it to perform the normal functions of living—sleeping, cooking, eating, among others.

No one function of living is definitive, however. Thus it is not sufficient to make premises a dwelling-house that someone sleeps there, unless he combines this with other living activities. At the end of the day it is a matter of common sense: are the premises in question someone's home? (*Curl* v. *Angelo* [1948] 2 All E.R. 189 (C.A.)).

The premises must be let *as* a dwelling: it is not sufficient that the tenant happens to use them for that purpose if they were in fact let for a different purpose (*Wolfe* v. *Hogan* [1949] 2 K.B. 194).

Furthermore, the premises must be let as a *separate* dwelling; in other words, the tenant must not be required to share any so-called essential living accommodation. If he shares only a room which is used for occasional purposes, a bathroom for example, the tenant will be protected, as he will when someone else is given such a limited right of access to one of the tenant's living rooms as not to constitute sharing at all (see above, pp. 62–4, and *Marsh* v. *Cooper* [1969] 1 W.L.R. 803 (C.A.)).

This requirement is qualified, however, by s.102(1) R.A. 1968, which provides that, where a tenant has exclusive possession of any accommodation which he holds on terms that include the use of other accommodation in common with another person or persons, not including the landlord, and but for this sharing, the tenant's separate accommodation would be let on or subject to a protected or statutory tenancy, the separate accommodation shall be deemed to be a dwelling-house let on a protected tenancy or subject to a statutory tenancy.

So long as the tenant has exclusive possession of at least one room, therefore, and does not share others with his landlord, he is within Part II. Section 101 covers the situation in which the tenant and landlord share, and provides that Part VI of the Act shall apply to the relationship, notwithstanding that the rent does not include any payment for the use of furniture or for services. The landlord need not, of course, be resident on the premises in order to share, but if he is resident at the relevant times then, regardless of whether he shares or not, the tenancy is not protected (see below).

Finally, the premises must be let as a *single* dwelling. If premises are let to a single tenant in order that he should be able to sub-let them as several dwellings, his tenancy is not protected, even though he occupies one of the dwellings himself (*Horford Investments Ltd* v. *Lambert* [1974] 1 All E.R. 131 (C.A.)).

ii. *The landlord*

Secondly, in order for the tenancy to be protected, the landlord must not be one of the following:

(*a*) The Crown;

(*b*) a local authority—'A local authority can get rid of a tenant if they do not like the colour of his eyes', according to LORD GODDARD C.J. in *Jenkins* v. *Paddington L.B.C.* [1954] J.P.L. 510 (D.C.), although, in practice, local authority tenants enjoy virtually total security, so long as they continue to observe the terms of the tenancy;

(*c*) A registered housing association (s.18 H.A. 1974, and see [1975] J.P.L. 71, 2);

(*d*) The Housing Corporation, a development corporation, the Commission for New Towns, or a charitable housing trust which provides the majority of its houses for the working classes;

(*e*) Resident. The circumstances in which the residence

of a landlord in a dwelling which forms part of the same premises as his tenant's dwelling will deprive that tenant of the protection he would otherwise have enjoyed are set out in s.5A Rent Act 1968. This section, which was added by Schedule 2 of the Rent Act 1974, is complex, and the precise scope and meaning of some of its terms and provisions must await clarification in the courts.

In order for s.5A to apply, the tenancy must have been granted on or after 14th August 1974, the commencement date of the Rent Act 1974. Next, the landlord must, at the time he grants the tenancy, occupy as his residence a dwelling-house forming part of the same building as that in which the tenant's dwelling is located. That is to say, the landlord must have his home in the same building. It is not sufficient, for example, that he retains a weekend flat or *pied-à-terre* in the building. A person can, however, have more than one residence, or home, although the courts tend to look with suspicion on such a claim (see, e.g. *Bevington* v. *Crawford* [1974] E. G. 191 (C.A.)).

It is not certain what is meant by 'building' in s.5A. It is clear, by virtue of s.5A(1)(*a*), that the term does *not* include a purpose-built block of flats. Beyond this it is not clear whether it comprehends single structures, such as a row of terrace houses all let by the same landlord, or is confined to such buildings as were originally self-contained dwellings, e.g. each individual house in the terrace. If the latter is correct, it may seem anomalous that a tenant who occupies a flat in the same house as the landlord is not protected, while those tenants who occupy identical flats on identical terms in the other houses in the terrace are protected.

A purpose-built block of flats is defined in s.5A(6) as a building which, as constructed, contained, and which still contains, two or more flats, a flat being a dwelling which forms part only of a building and is separated horizontally from another dwelling which forms part of the same building.

The test of a landlord's 'occupying as a residence' is the same as that applied to a statutory tenant (s.5A(7)). This is considered below (p. 118).

The landlord, who, as we have seen, must be resident when he grants the tenancy, must continue in residence at all times thereafter if the tenancy is to fall outside Part II, except that certain periods of absence from residence during the tenancy are discounted, under the complicated provisions of s.5A(2). Casual absences, such as a holiday, which do not involve giving up residence, presumably do not signify at all.

These excepted periods are first, any period of not more than fourteen days beginning with the date on which the interest of the landlord under the tenancy becomes vested in law and in equity in an individual who, during that period, does not occupy as his residence another dwelling forming part of the building concerned.

Second, if, within this fourteen-day period, that individual notifies the tenant in writing of his intention to occupy as his residence another dwelling in the same building, the excepted period is that beginning with the date on which the interest of the landlord under the tenancy becomes vested in law and in equity in that individual (i.e. the beginning of the fourteen-day period) and ending at the *earliest* of the three following times:

(*a*) at the expiry of a period of six months beginning on that date;

(*b*) on the date on which the landlord's interest ceases to be so vested; or

(*c*) on the date when the new landlord takes up his residence in a dwelling in the same building.

Third, any period of not more than twelve months beginning with the date on which the interest of the landlord becomes, and during which it remains, vested in one of the following, is discounted:

(*a*) the personal representatives of a deceased person, acting in that capacity; or

(*b*) trustees as such; or

(*c*) the Probate Judge, by virtue of s.9 of the Administration of Estates Act 1925.

During any such period of absence from residence, possession can only be recovered from a tenant on the grounds applicable to a regulated tenancy (below, pp. 120–5). In other words, a tenant is as secure against eviction during the permitted absence from residence of his landlord as a regulated tenant (s.5A(4) R.A. 1968).

A tenancy which is prevented from being a protected tenancy only because of the resident landlord exception is to be treated as a Part VI contract (below, pp. 125–8), notwithstanding that the rent does not include any payment for the use of furniture or for services (s.102A R.A. 1968, added by Schedule 2, Part II para. 4 R.A. 1974).

The resident landlord exception does not apply to a tenancy granted to someone who, immediately beforehand, was a protected or statutory tenant of *any* dwelling in the same building. Nor does it apply to a tenancy for a term of years certain granted to someone who, immediately beforehand, was an *unprotected* tenant of any dwelling in the same building, if he was only unprotected because his prior tenancy *was* within the resident landlord exception.

A term of years includes a term for less than a year, or for a year or years and a fraction of a year, or from year to year: s.206(xxvii) Law of Property Act 1925.

iii. *Excluded tenancies*

Certain types of tenancy are not protected under Part II R.A. 1968. These include:

(*a*) A tenancy of a dwelling let at a rent which includes payments in respect of board or attendance (s.2(1) (*b*) R.A. 1968, as amended).

Attendance has been defined as a 'service personal to the tenant performed by an attendant provided by the landlord in accordance with his covenant for the benefit or convenience of the individual tenant in his use or enjoyment of the demised premises' (*per* VISCOUNT SIMON in *Palser* v. *Grinling* [1948] A.C. 291 at 310 (H.L.); as to board, see above, p. 100).

Attendance is not relevant, however, unless the amount of rent which is fairly attributable to attendance, having regard to the value of the attendance to the tenant, forms a substantial part of the rent (s.2(3) R.A. 1968, as amended).

It should be noted, however, that even insubstantial *board* will suffice to except a tenancy from Part II protection.

(*b*) Agricultural holdings and lettings partly for business purposes. These are subject to different legislation and are outside the scope of this book.

(*c*) A tenancy which is granted by an educational institution or body of persons, specified by statutory instrument, to a person who is pursuing or intends to pursue a course of study provided by a specified educational institution or body (s.2(1) (*bb*) R.A. 1968, as amended).

The landlord and the institution or body providing the course of study need not be the same.

(*d*) A holiday letting (s.2(1)(*bbb*) R.A. 1968, as amended).

(*e*) A tenancy at a low rent. This is a tenancy under which no rent, or no quantifiable rent, is payable, or the rent payable is less than two-thirds of the rateable value of the dwelling on 23rd March 1965, or such later date as the dwelling (or the building of which it forms part) first entered the valuation list. This is the so-called appropriate day (s.6(3) R.A. 1968).

However, if the appropriate day for a particular dwelling falls before 22nd March 1973 and on its appropriate day the dwelling had a rateable value in excess of £400 if the dwelling is in Greater London, or £200 elsewhere, the rent must be less than two-thirds of the rateable value on 22nd March 1973 in order for the tenancy not to be protected (Schedule 5 para. 11(1) Counter-Inflation Act 1973).

If the tenancy relates to a part only of a rated building, the rateable value of that part is to be determined by a proper apportionment, and any dispute as to this is to be resolved by the County court, whose decision is final (s.6(1) R.A. 1968, and see *R.* v. *Westminster (City) L.B.C. Rent Officer, ex parte Rendall* [1973] 3 All E.R. 119 (C.A.)).

If, however, the tenancy is in all other respects a *controlled* tenancy (below, pp. 116–7) it will still be protected if the rent, though less than two-thirds of the rateable value on the appropriate day, is nevertheless at least two-thirds of the rateable value in 1939 (if the dwelling was brought into control by the Rent and Mortgage Interest Restrictions Act 1939) or at least two-thirds of the 1914 rateable value (if the dwelling was brought into control by the Increase of Rent and Mortgage Interest (Restrictions) Act 1920) (s.7(3), Sched. 2, Part II R.A. 1968).

(*f*) A tenancy which includes agricultural land of more than two acres (s.2(1)(*c*) R.A. 1968).

iv. *Rateable value limits*

The rateable value of the dwelling on the appropriate day

(above, p. 115) must fall *below* the ceilings specified by s.1(1) R.A. 1968, as amended by s.14 Counter-Inflation Act 1973, if the tenancy is to come within Part II. The appropriate day, as we have seen, is 23rd March, or such later date as the premises in question were first rated.

However, a tenancy will be *controlled*, regardless of the rateable value of the relevant dwelling on the appropriate day, if it satisfies the other requirements of a controlled tenancy (see below) and the rateable value of the dwelling did not exceed £40 in the Metropolitan Police District or the City of London, or £30 elsewhere on 7th November 1956 (Sched. 2, para. 1(*a*) R.A. 1968).

In all other cases, a tenancy of a dwelling for which the appropriate day falls between 23rd March 1965 and 21st March 1973 is protected unless the rateable value of that dwelling exceeds *all three* of the following figures:

(*a*) £400/£200 on the appropriate day;

(*b*) £600/£300 on 22nd March 1973; and

(*c*) £1500/£750 on 1st April 1973.

If the dwelling was first rated between 22nd March 1973 and 31st March 1973, a tenancy of that dwelling is protected unless the rateable value exceeds *both* the following figures:

(*a*) £600/£300 on the appropriate day; and

(*b*) £1500/£750 on 1st April 1973

If the dwelling was first rated on or after 1st April 1973, a tenancy of that dwelling is protected unless the rateable value on the appropriate day exceeds £1500 in Greater London or £750 elsewhere.

c. Controlled tenancies

A tenancy is controlled if:

(*a*) the dwelling is within the rateable value limit, on 7th November 1956 (see above);

(*b*) the dwelling was provided (whether by construction or conversion) before 30th August 1954. If the dwelling was produced by work begun after 29th August 1954, or work begun before that date but completed after it, a tenancy of that dwelling will still be controlled if the work was done with a grant payable under the Housing Act 1949 or the Housing (Financial Provisions) Act 1958;

(*c*) the tenancy is not a long tenancy, i.e. for a term in excess of twenty-one years;

(*d*) the tenancy was created by a lease or agreement which came into operation before 6th July 1957;

(*e*) the tenancy has not been converted into a regulated tenancy, under the provisions of the Housing Finance Act 1972 (see s.8 R.A. 1968).

d. Statutory tenancies

i. *Nature of a statutory tenancy*

Upon the termination of a protected tenancy, the person who, immediately beforehand, was the protected tenant, becomes the statutory tenant, and has the same security of tenure as he enjoyed before termination, for as long as he continues to occupy the dwelling as his home (s.3(1)(*a*) R.A. 1968).

A so-called statutory tenancy is in fact simply a personal right given to the former protected tenant to remain in his home. It is not a right in property and so cannot be assigned or bequeathed, although it can pass to designated individuals in the limited circumstances envisaged in Schedule I.

The terms and conditions of the contractual tenancy, insofar as they are consistent with statutory requirements, continue into the statutory tenancy (s.12(1) R.A. 1968). The statutory tenant, like the protected tenant, is obliged to allow the landlord access to the dwelling and all reasonable facilities for carrying out any repairs to the dwelling which the landlord is entitled to make (above, pp. 15–26).

A landlord is entitled to the same notice to quit from a statutory tenant as was provided for in the contractual tenancy. By virtue of s.16 Rent Act 1957 (a provision which is expressly saved by s.12(5) R.A. 1968) this must be at least four weeks' notice. If no period of notice is specified in the contract, then the statutory tenant must give not less than three months' notice (s.12(3)).

It is an offence for a statutory tenant to ask for or accept any consideration from anyone other than the landlord as a condition of giving up possession of the dwelling (s.13(1) R.A. 1968). Moreover, if the statutory tenant requires that any articles, including furniture, be bought as a condition of giving up possession, any sum in excess of a reasonable price for those articles is treated as an illegal consideration under s.13(1). The offence is punishable by a fine of up to £100.

ii. *Loss of protection by absence*

If the tenant ceases to keep the premises as his home, he loses his rights as a statutory tenant, although temporary absences will not deprive him of protection. If an absence is protracted, however, the burden may fall upon the tenant to prove that he is still making his home in the dwelling. This he can only do by retaining upon the premises some symbol of continued residence, e.g. a caretaker or furniture, as well as by maintaining the intention to return. If the symbol is removed, albeit without the tenant's knowledge or desire, protection is lost. In *Brown* v. *Brash & Ambrose* [1948] 2 K.B. 247 (C.A.) the tenant was imprisoned, leaving his mistress in occupation; she abandoned the premises and protection was lost (see also *Bevington* v. *Crawford* [1974] E. G. 191; *Skinner* v. *Geary* [1931] 2 K.B. 546 (C.A.) and *Roland House Gardens Ltd* v. *Cravitz*, *The Times* 12th December 1974).

An intention to occupy premises as a residence *in the future* will not suffice to protect the statutory tenant (*Walker* v. *Ogilvy* (1974) 28 P. & C.R. 288 (C.A.)).

iii. *Transmission of statutory tenancy*

On the death of the original tenant, that is, the person who immediately before his death was a protected tenant, or a statutory tenant by virtue of his previous tenancy, the statutory tenancy can be transmitted to the original tenant's widow, if she was residing with him at the time of his death; or, if there is no widow, to a member of the original tenant's family who was residing with him at the time of his death, and for at least six months immediately beforehand. If there is more than one such person, they must agree among themselves (the landlord having no voice in the matter) and, in default of agreement, the County court shall select which one of them is to be statutory tenant.

The successors to the original tenant are themselves only protected for so long as they continue to occupy the dwelling as their home.

A statutory tenancy may be transmitted no more than twice. If a new protected tenancy is granted to the first successor, the new tenancy can be transmitted only once; if granted to a second successor, then not at all.

Whether or not one person is residing with another is a question of fact (see, e.g. *Foreman* v. *Beagley* [1969] 1 W.L.R. 1387 (C.A.); *Morgan* v. *Murch* [1970] 1 W.L.R. 778 (C.A.)). People may still be residing together although one of them is absent from the premises for a protracted period, e.g. because he is in hospital. It seems clear, however, that an occupant is not residing with a tenant if that occupant has been installed simply in order to maintain the tenant's technical continuity of residence during a prolonged absence.

It is also difficult to determine the precise scope of the phrase 'member of the original tenant's family'. Although it has been given a relatively wide interpretation in the courts, it is not as comprehensive as 'household'. It seems clear, however, that all children are included, and 'not only legitimate children but also step-children, illegitimate children, and adopted children, whether adopted in due form or not' (*per* DENNING L.J. in *Brock* v. *Wollams* [1949] 2 K.B. 388 at p. 396

(C.A.)). Indeed, some authorities regard children as the key-note of a family. Certainly it has been held that a 'common-law' spouse is not 'family' unless there are children of the union (*Gammans* v. *Ekins* [1950] 2 K.B. 328 (C.A.)). According to ASQUITH L.J. in this case, 'the material decisions limit membership of the same family to three relationships: first, that of children; secondly, those constituted by way of legitimate marriage, and thirdly, relationships whereby one person becomes in *loco parentis* to another'.

e. Loss of security of tenure

A landlord can recover possession of premises let on a protected tenancy or subject to a statutory tenancy only in the limited circumstances envisaged by s.10 and Schedule 3 of the Rent Act 1968, as amended, and then only with an order of the court.

Section 10(2) provides that a possession order *must* be made if the landlord's claim falls within one of the categories set out in Schedule 3, Part II (below, pp. 123–4). Section 10(1) gives the court a discretion whether or not to make the order when the landlord's claim falls within Schedule 3, Part I.

i. *Cases where the court has a discretion to order possession*

The grounds for possession under Sched, 3, Part I are:

Case 1: Failure to pay rent, or breach of any other obligation of the tenancy.

Case 2: Nuisance or annoyance caused to an adjoining occupier by the tenant, anyone residing or lodging with the tenant, or a sub-tenant.

A landlord may also recover possession under Case 2 if the tenant, resident, lodger, or sub-tenant has been convicted of using the dwelling, or allowing it to be used, for immoral or illegal purposes (*Abrahams* v. *Wilson* [1971] 2 Q.B. 88 (C.A.)).

Case 3: Deterioration in the condition of the dwelling through acts of waste by, or the neglect or default of, the tenant, anyone residing or lodging with him, or a sub-tenant. If either a lodger or sub-tenant is responsible, however, no order will be made unless the court is satisfied that the tenant has failed to take whatever reasonable steps were available to him to remove the culprit.

Case 3A (added by Sched. 1, Part I, para. 1, R.A. 1974): This is in substantially the same terms as Case 3, except that it relates to deterioration, caused by ill-treatment, in the condition of any furniture supplied under the tenancy.

Case 4: The tenant has given notice to quit and the landlord has, in consequence, contracted to sell or let the dwelling, or has taken any other steps as a result of which he would be seriously prejudiced if he could not obtain possession.

Case 5: The tenant has assigned or sublet the whole dwelling, or has sublet part when the rest was already sublet, after the relevant date and without the landlord's consent. The relevant date for controlled tenancies is 1st September 1939; for unfurnished regulated tenancies it is 8th December 1965, unless the tenancy is regulated by virtue of s.14 of the Counter-Inflation Act 1973, in which case the relevant date is 22nd March 1973; and for furnished regulated tenancies it is 14th August 1974.

Case 6: Relates to controlled tenancies of premises with an off-licence, and is beyond the scope of this book.

Case 7: The tenant was, but is no longer, employed by the landlord or a former landlord, as a result of which the dwelling was let to him, and the landlord now reasonably requires the dwelling as a residence for a full-time employee of his own or of a tenant. It is sufficient that a contract of employment has been made which is conditional upon a house being provided for the prospective employee.

If a landlord obtains possession of premises under Case 7 by misrepresenting or concealing material facts, the court can order him to compensate the tenant for his loss (s.19 R.A. 1968).

Case 8: The landlord reasonably requires the dwelling for his own home, or as a home for an adult child, or for the landlord's father or mother, or (if the tenancy is regulated) for his father-in-law or mother-in-law.

Case 8 can be invoked only if the landlord became landlord by buying the dwelling, or an interest in it, before 24th March 1965 (if the premises are subject to an unfurnished regulated tenancy not brought into protection by s.14 of the Counter-Inflation Act 1973) or 8th March 1973 (a s.14 tenancy) or 24th May 1974 (a furnished regulated tenancy) or 7th November 1956 (a controlled tenancy) (see *Thomas* v. *Fryer* [1970] 1 W.L.R. 845 (C.A.)).

No order will be made under Case 8 if the court considers that, in all the circumstances, greater hardship would be caused by making the order than by refusing it. As under Case 7, the court can order a landlord to pay compensation to the tenant if possession has been obtained by the misrepresentation or concealment of material facts.

Case 9: The tenant has overcharged any protected or statutory sub-tenant, or any sub-tenant who holds under a Part VI contract. Overcharging is determined by reference to the maximum rent provisions of Parts III, V, or VI of the 1968 Act, as appropriate.

ii. *Postponement or suspension of a Part I order*

Where an order has been made in a Part I case, the court can suspend execution of the order, or postpone the date of possession, and any such suspension or postponement can be made subject to whatever conditions, concerning matters such as payment of rent arrears, the court deems appropriate. The court also has the power to cancel the possession order altogether if such conditions are satisfied (s.11 R.A. 1968).

Only the actual tenant, and not his spouse, can apply to stay or suspend the possession order, but an application can be made even after the time fixed by the court for the tenant to surrender possession has passed (*Penn* v. *Dunn* [1970] 2 Q.B. 686 (C.A.)).

iii. *Cases where the court must order possession*

If the landlord can bring himself within any of the following cases, which are laid down in Sched. 3, Part II, the court *must* order immediate possession:

Case 10: This enables a person who lets his home on a regulated tenancy to recover possession, provided that he requires it for his home once more, or as a home for any member of his family who resided with him when the landlord last had his home in the dwelling.

Although there is a requirement that the landlord give the tenant written notice, not later than the relevant date, that possession might be recovered on this ground, the court can now waive this requirement. Similarly, the court can waive the requirement that the dwelling must not have been let on a protected tenancy after 8th December 1965, without such a notice having been given (s.3(3) R.A. 1974).

The relevant date for a regulated furnished tenancy which was created before 14th August 1974, is 13th February 1975. For any other protected tenancy which was created before 8th December 1965, the relevant date is 7th July 1966. In any other case the relevant date is the date on which the tenancy began.

The Rent Act 1974 adds three new cases to Sched. 3, Part II R.A. 1968:

Case 10A: This enables a person who has acquired a dwelling-house as a retirement home, and who meantime has let it on a regulated tenancy, to recover possession upon his retirement. If he dies, a member of his family who was residing with him at the time of his death can recover it on the landlord's death. This Case is subject to similar conditions as to the giving of notice as Case 10: that is, the landlord must have given written notice by the relevant date that possession might be recovered for this reason, and not, since 14th August 1974, have let the dwelling on a protected tenancy without giving such a notice. As in Case 10, however, the court can waive either or both of these conditions, if satisfied that it is just and equitable to make a possession order.

Case 10B: This provides for the recovery of possession of a dwelling let on a fixed term protected tenancy of not more than eight months, provided that, at some time within the year preceding the relevant date, the dwelling was occupied under a holiday tenancy or licence, and, not later than the relevant date, the landlord notified the tenant in writing that possession might be recovered for this reason.

Case 10C: This is analogous, permitting recovery of possession where the dwelling is let on a fixed term not exceeding twelve months, having been subject to a student letting of the type specified in s.2(1)(*bb*) (above, p. 114) within the twelve months preceding the relevant date. Written notice must have been given to the tenant, as under Cases 10, 10A, and 10B. There is no discretion to waive the giving of notice under either Case 10B or 10C.

The remaining Cases, 11, 12, and 13, deal with situations which are not directly relevant to the subject of this book.

iv. *Recovery of possession where suitable alternative accommodation is available*

If the landlord cannot bring himself within one of the specific situations in Schedule 3, he might nevertheless recover possession if the court thinks it reasonable to make an order, and it is satisfied that suitable alternative accommodation is available for the tenant or will be available for him when the order takes effect (s.10(1)(*a*) R.A. 1968).

Suitable alternative accommodation is defined in Schedule 3, Part IV, as amended. A certificate from a local authority, stating that suitable alternative accommodation will be provided by them for the tenant, by a specified date, is sufficient to fulfil the requirement of s.10(1)(*a*). Otherwise the court must be satisfied that the alternative accommodation will be:

(*a*) let to the tenant on a protected tenancy or on such terms as will give reasonably equivalent security;

(*b*) reasonably suitable to the tenant and his family as regards proximity to work;

(*c*) *either* comparable in respect of rent and size to accommodation provided in that area for similar families by the local authority, *or* reasonably suitable to the tenant's means and his family's needs regarding size and character; and

(*d*) if any furniture was provided under the tenancy, supplied with furniture that is *either* similar to that provided, *or* reasonably suitable to the needs of the tenant and his family: Sched. 1, Part I, para. 7 R.A. 1974.

Part of the dwelling presently let to the tenant can constitute suitable alternative accommodation (*Mykolyshyn* v. *Noah* [1970] 1 W.L.R. 1271 (C.A.), cf. *MacDonnell* v. *Daly* [1969] 1 W.L.R. 1482 (C.A.)).

2. Security of tenure under Part VI, Rent Act 1968

The nature of a Part VI contract has already been outlined (above, pp. 96–100). It remains to consider the extent to which a tenant holding under a Part VI contract is secure from eviction.

a. Dispossession by court order only

The first point to note is that the tenant cannot be dispossessed without a court order, even after the expiry of his tenancy, so long as he continues to make his home in at least a part of the dwelling. This is the basic security available to any residential tenant who is unprotected by Part II of the 1968 Act (s.32 R.A. 1965).

b. Extension of notice to quit

Additional security is available to Part VI tenants only if

and when a notice to quit has been served. Hence there is no additional security when the tenancy automatically lapses at the end of a fixed term.

Unlike Part II security, the right to hold over after a notice to quit does not arise automatically, but must be granted by a rent tribunal. The security takes the form of an extension of the notice to quit, rather than as a separate statutory right arising after the contractual period has ended.

The Rent Act 1968 envisages two situations in which a rent tribunal can grant an extension of tenure:

i. *Notice to quit served after reference to rent tribunal*

Under s.72 R.A. 1968 a lessor, lessee, or local authority can refer a Part VI contract to a rent tribunal for consideration of the proper rent payable, and the tribunal's decision, approving, reducing, or increasing the contract rent must be registered by the local authority. After registration the lessor, lessee, or local authority can ask the tribunal to reconsider the rent in the light of changed circumstances (s.75 R.A. 1968).

Section 77 provides for the situation in which either the lessee or the local authority has applied to the rent tribunal under s.72 or s.75, and the lessor thereafter serves a notice to quit. If that notice is served in the period between the application to the tribunal and six months after its decision, the notice cannot take effect before six months from the decision. This is subject to four exceptions or qualifications:

(*a*) if the tribunal thinks fit, it can substitute a shorter period than six months (s.77(2)(*a*) R.A. 1968).

(*b*) if the local authority or the lessee withdraws the reference of the contract rent to the tribunal, the notice to quit takes effect seven days after withdrawal (s.77(2)(*b*) R.A. 1968).

(*c*) if the lessor occupied the dwelling as a residence before the Part VI contract was made (and so is called the owner-occupier for this purpose) *and*, on or before the letting (or by 7th June 1966 if the letting was before 8th December 1965) the lessor notified the lessee in writing that he was owner-occupier, *and* the lessor does not have his home in another part of the same house, *and* the dwelling is now required as a home for the lessor or a member of his family who resided with him when he last had his home there, the rent tribunal cannot postpone operation of the notice to quit (s.79 R.A. 1968).

(*d*) after the tribunal has granted a suspension of the notice to quit, the lessor can apply to the tribunal to reduce the period during which the notice is to be inoperative. The tribunal may reduce the period by which they originally suspended the notice if the lessee has broken the terms of the contract, or if he, or his lodger, or someone residing with him has been a nuisance or annoyance to adjoining neighbours, or has been convicted of using the dwelling or allowing the dwelling to be used for an immoral or an illegal purpose, or if the condition of the dwelling, or of any furniture provided for the lessee's use under the contract, has deteriorated, owing to acts, neglect, or ill-treatment by the lessee, someone residing with him, or his lodger (s.80(2) R.A. 1968, as amended by s.8(2) R.A. 1974).

ii. *Notice to quit served without previous reference to rent tribunal and further extensions of notice to quit*

The provisions of s.78 overlap with those of s.77, in that s.78 applies both when s.77 has already been invoked or when the notice to quit is served *before* any reference to the rent tribunal, so that s.77 is inapplicable.

In either case, during the currency of the notice to quit or the period of extension granted under s.77, the lessee can ask the rent tribunal to extend the period of the notice to quit still further. The tribunal can then grant an extension or further extension of up to six months beyond the date on which the notice to quit would otherwise have taken effect. The lessee can continue to apply under s.78 and receive extensions of up to six months, provided he applies before the period of the previous extension has expired and the notice to quit thus become effective.

The tribunal cannot grant an extension under s.78 if the original six months was reduced on the application of the lessor under s.80. Furthermore, since s.80 also applies to an extension under s.78, once a s.78 extension has been reduced for default by the lessee, someone residing with him, or his lodger, no further extensions can be granted.

Before the Rent Act 1974, an extension could not be granted under s.78 if the original extension under s.77 was for less than six months, but this limitation has now been removed (s.8(1) R.A. 1974).

3. Security of tenure under Part III Rent Act 1965

As has been noted, s.32 Rent Act 1965 provides the basic minimum protection for residential tenants who hold over after the termination of their tenancy. So long as the tenant continues to reside in at least a part of the premises, he can only be removed by court order; otherwise, his dispossession is an offence under s.30(1) R.A. 1965 (below, pp. 144–5); *Warder* v. *Cooper* above, p. 101).

4. Sub-tenancies

a. The nature of a sub-tenancy

A sub-tenant is the tenant of a landlord who is himself the tenant of a superior landlord. As between the sub-tenant and his landlord (the head tenant) the relationship is, basically, a normal landlord and tenant relationship. Thus, references in the Rent Act 1968 to landlord, tenant, tenancy, and let, also comprehend a sub-tenancy, unless the particular context requires a different interpretation (s.113(1) R.A. 1968).

b. The sub-tenant's security of tenure

A sub-tenant's security of tenure is not only at risk from his immediate landlord, however, but also from the head landlord. The sub-tenant's position when the head tenancy (i.e. his own landlord's tenancy) is determined in considered in s.18 R.A. 1968.

If the head landlord obtains a possession order on either of the discretionary grounds specified in s.10(1) R.A. 1968 (i.e. because he is within one of the Sched. 3 Part I Cases, or because suitable alternative accommodation is available for the tenant, and, in either case, the court thinks it reasonable to make an order) the order will not give the head landlord a right of possession against any lawful sub-tenant, whether he is sub-tenant of the whole or part only of the dwelling. The head landlord must therefore proceed separately against the sub-tenant, or join him as defendant in the proceedings against the head tenant and, in either case, establish a right to possession as against the sub-tenant (s.18(1) R.A. 1968).

The position of the sub-tenant in relation to the head landlord, after the head tenancy has been determined, for whatever reason, depends on whether or not the head tenancy was protected (or statutory).

If the head tenancy was protected or statutory, the lawful sub-tenant is deemed to become the tenant of the head landlord on the same terms as he would have held from the head tenant if the head tenant's protected or statutory tenancy had continued (s.18(2) R.A. 1968). (Section 18(2) does not, however, apply to an *unlawful* sub-tenancy; as against the head landlord, the unlawful sub-tenant is a trespasser.) Hence, if the sub-tenancy was also protected or statutory, it will remain so, and, presumably, the head landlord will only be able to recover possession against the sub-tenant for reasons that would have been available to the head tenant.

c. Head tenancy unfurnished; sub-tenancy furnished

However, if the head tenancy was unfurnished, and the sub-tenancy is furnished, the head landlord is not required to provide furniture (or services) if he notifies the sub-tenant, within six weeks of determining the head tenancy, that no furniture or services will be provided (s.13 R.A. 1974).

d. Long head tenancy

A long head tenancy (i.e. over twenty-one years) at a low rent which, apart from the low rent, would have been protected, is treated as protected for the purposes of s.18(2), unless the long tenancy, at the moment that the sub-tenancy was created, was subject to a notice to terminate under s.4(1) of the Landlord and Tenant Act 1954, or was being continued under s.3(1) of that Act: s.18(4) R.A. 1968.

e. Head tenancy neither protected nor statutory

If the head tenancy was *not* protected or statutory, then s.18(5) R.A. 1968 operates. This provides that, where there is a protected or statutory sub-tenancy of a dwelling which forms part of premises not let on a protected tenancy, then on determination of the superior tenancy, the dwelling is to be treated as if it had been separately let direct to the sub-tenant by the head landlord, but for the same purposes as the head tenancy, and at a rent which is a just proportion of that payable under the head tenancy. Unlike subs.(2), subs.(5) appears to apply even though the sub-tenancy is unlawful.

It has been decided that this provision only applies where the head tenancy is of a dwelling-house (*Maunsell* v. *Olins* [1975] 1 All E.R. 16 (H.L.)). The sub-tenant will enjoy continued protection only on the assumption that, if the head landlord had been the sub-tenant's landlord from the outset, his tenancy would have been protected. Protection will not continue, therefore, if the landlord falls within one of the excepted category of landlords (above, pp. 110–3). Moreover, since the notional separate letting is deemed to be for the like purposes as under the superior letting, those purposes must also be consistent with a protected tenancy. When *Maunsell* v. *Olins* was before the Court of Appeal, LAWTON L.J. suggested that the purpose of section 18(5) was to maintain protection for sub-tenants residing in large houses let on a head lease to developers. If, however, the object of the head lease is non-residential, it would seem to follow that the sub-lease is no longer in fact protected once the head lease is determined.

5. Rent books

a. The right to a rent book

The lawful residential occupant of any premises for which rent is payable on a *weekly* basis is entitled to a rent book, or similar document, from the person who granted him the right of occupation, unless board is supplied and the value of that board to the tenant represents a substantial part of the whole rent (s.1 Landlord and Tenant Act 1962).

b. Information to be included in the rent book

The rent book must contain certain specified information. We have already seen that s.81 H.A. 1957 requires that a summary of s.77 (definition of overcrowding), s.78 (offences in relation to overcrowding) and s.80 (power of local authorities to licence overcrowding) and a statement of the permitted maximum number of occupants be included in every rent book or similar document.

In addition, the Rent Book (Forms of Notice) Regulations 1972 (S.I. 1972 no. 1827; S.I. 1973 no. 1055) require the inclusion of the name and address of the landlord and the landlord's agent; the address of the dwelling; the rent, and whether or not it includes rates; a summary of the law applicable before and after a rent has been registered; a summary of the law relating to security of tenure and harassment; and a summary of the local authority rent allowance scheme (below, Chapter 10).

Failure to comply with these requirements is a summary offence, punishable by a maximum fine of £50 on first conviction, and a maximum fine of £100 for a subsequent conviction (s.4(3) Landlord and Tenant Act 1962).

6. Premiums and payments

a. Premiums ('Key money')

A premium is any pecuniary consideration other than the rent (s.92(1) R.A. 1968). It is an offence, punishable by a fine of up to £100, for any person to require or receive the payment of a premium as a condition of granting, renewing or continuing a protected tenancy, or a Part VI contract in respect of which a rent has been registered. It is also an offence for a landlord to require a payment to be made to a third party (s.85(1), (2); *Elmdene Estates Ltd* v. *White* [1960] A.C. 528 (H.L.)).

The convicting court can order the premium to be repaid, or the person who paid the premium can bring proceedings in the County court, regardless of amount, for its recovery (ss.85(4), 87(5) R.A. 1968).

b. Payments for furniture

Moreover, if any furniture is bought as a condition of being granted a protected tenancy or a Part VI contract in respect of which a rent has been registered, or as a condition of having it renewed or continued, any amount in excess of a reasonable price for that furniture is regarded as an illegal premium (s.88 R.A. 1968). Although, in the typical situation, the furniture will be bought from the landlord by the incoming tenant, s.88 is not confined to this situation. It is equally an offence if the furniture is bought by or from a third party.

It is a further offence, punishable by a fine of up to £100, to *offer* furniture for sale at a price which the offeror knows or ought to know is unreasonably high, if the offer is made in connection with the proposed grant, renewal, or continuance of a protected tenancy, or a Part VI contract in respect of which a rent has been registered.

c. Payment in consideration of giving up possession

A statutory tenant commits an analogous offence, punishable by a fine of up to £100, if he asks for or receives any consideration, whether in money or otherwise, from anyone other than the landlord, as a condition of giving up possession of the dwelling. Moreover, if the statutory tenant requires that furniture or other articles be bought, as a condition of giving up possession, any amount in excess of a reasonable price for those articles is to be treated as an illegal consideration. On conviction the offender can be required to repay the value of the illegal consideration (i.e. the excess over a reasonable price).

7. Notice to quit

We have already noted that both landlord and tenant are entitled to a minimum of four weeks' notice to quit (s.16 R.A. 1957). In addition, the notice must be in writing and contain such information as may be prescribed by statutory instrument (s.16 R.A. 1957, as amended by s.123 H.A. 1974).

8. Spouses and co-habitees

This section considers the rights of occupation of a spouse or co-habitee, when the home is held under a tenancy by the other partner. This matter has two aspects: the right to remain or be reinstated in the dwelling, and the right to exclude the other partner from it. The law in these areas is a complex pattern of statutory and common law provisions. With regard to the question of injunctive relief it is particularly difficult to offer an accurate summary of the law, since there are different views upon the circumstances in which an injunction may be granted, and the law seems presently to be in a state of flux.

a. Rights during the subsistence of marriage

i. *Statutory rights of occupation*

Section 1(1) of the Matrimonial Homes Act 1967 gives certain rights of occupation to a spouse who is not otherwise entitled to occupy the matrimonial home under any contract or statute, or by virtue of any estate or interest in the dwelling.

These rights are as follows: the right, if in occupation, not to be evicted or excluded from the dwelling or any part of it by the other spouse, except with the leave of the court; and the right, if not in occupation, to enter into and occupy the dwelling. This latter right can only be exercised with the leave of the court.

A spouse therefore has an independent right to occupy the matrimonial home during the subsistence of the marriage. Even if the other spouse, the tenant, is prepared to surrender the tenancy, the landlord cannot obtain possession against the spouse who is protected by s.1(1). So long as he (or, more usually, she) continues to fulfil the obligations of the tenancy, the tenancy is kept alive (*Middleton* v. *Baldock (T.W.)* [1950] 1 K.B. 657 (C.A.)).

ii. *Modification of possession order*

There is a hiatus in this protection, however. If the tenancy is protected or statutory and the landlord obtains a possession order, the tenant alone can apply to have execution of the order suspended or delayed under s.11 R.A. 1968. The other spouse must make out a case for suspension or delay when the court hears the landlord's application. Thereafter it will be too late (*Penn* v. *Dunn* [1970] 2 Q.B. 686 (C.A.)).

iii. *Modification and termination of rights of occupation*

Section 1(2) provides that, so long as one spouse has rights of occupation, *either* may apply to the court for an order declaring, enforcing, restricting, or terminating those rights, or regulating the exercise by either spouse of the right to occupy the dwelling.

The only rights which can be *terminated* under this provision are those given in subsection (1). The spouse who occupies the dwelling by virtue of any estate or interest, or under a contract or enactment other than s.1(1) itself, may apply to have the other's s.1(1) rights terminated, but the otherwise unprotected spouse cannot. Nor does the court's jurisdiction to regulate the exercise by *either* spouse of the right to occupy extend to barring either one from the dwelling. Regulation stops short of exclusion (*Tarr* v. *Tarr* [1973] A.C. 254 (H.L.)).

iv. *Exclusion from the matrimonial home*

The rights of occupation given by s.1(1) M.H.A. 1967 do not include the right to bar the other spouse from the matrimonial home. A court has no jurisdiction under the Act to issue an injunction excluding from the matrimonial home a spouse who has the right, apart from s.1(1), to occupy it.

A court may, however, enjoin a spouse, if necessary banning him or her from the matrimonial home, when the physical or mental health of the other spouse, or their children, is at risk. It is not clear that this can be done unless the injunction is ancillary to other proceedings, such as a petition for divorce or separation. Certainly an injunction can only be obtained in a *County* court if other proceedings have been instigated (*R.* v. *Cheshire County Judge etc, ex parte Malone* [1921] 2 K.B. 694 (C.A.)). In theory, an injunction can be obtained in the *High* Court even though no other relief is sought (s.45 Supreme Court of Judicature (Consolidation) Act 1925), but judges appear to be reluctant to exercise this jurisdiction independently of related proceedings (*Phillips* v. *Phillips* [1973] 1 W.L.R. 615 (C.A.); *Bassett* v. *Bassett* [1975] 1 All E.R. 513 (C.A.), each of which contains *dicta* suggesting that the jurisdiction can be exercised whenever there is a threat to health, regardless of whether other proceedings are in prospect).

b. The position upon divorce

It is not the purpose of this book to examine in any detail the complicated provisions for readjustment of property rights between spouses upon divorce, nullity, or separation.

However, two statutory provisions are of particular relevance to the present subject:

i. *Transfer of protected or statutory tenancy between spouses*

Section 7, M.H.A. 1967 enacts that a court which grants a decree of divorce or nullity may order a *protected* or *statutory tenancy* to be transferred from one spouse to the other. Such a transfer may be ordered at any time between decree nisi and decree absolute, but it takes effect only as from the date of decree absolute.

Where the tenancy is protected (i.e. the tenancy agreement is still in force, above, p. 117) the order operates to vest the former tenant spouse's estate or interest in the other party, with all attendant rights and liabilities.

If the tenancy is statutory, (i.e., a merely personal right and no longer an estate or interest) the order takes the form of a direction that the former tenant spouse shall cease to be entitled to occupy the dwelling and that his or her former spouse shall be deemed to be the tenant or the sole tenant, as the case may be, under the statutory tenancy.

The court may at the same time direct that both spouses shall be liable to discharge any outstanding liabilities under the tenancy (e.g. arrears of rent) although originally only one spouse, the tenant, was liable.

The landlord has a right to be heard by the court before an order of transfer is made.

The former tenant spouse cannot be banned from the matrimonial home under this provision before the decree is made absolute, since he or she remains the tenant (or joint tenant) until that time. An injunction to restrain a threatened trespass can be obtained against that spouse, however, at the time when the transfer is ordered, although it will not take effect until decree absolute (*Maynard* v. *Maynard* [1969] P. 88).

It will be noticed that s.7 M.H.A. 1967 only applies to protected and statutory tenancies. There was thought to be little point in including tenancies which offer no real security of tenure (Morton Committee Cmnd 9678 para. 687 (iii)). However, Part VI contracts are not included, although they offer limited security. While council tenancies are not subject to s.7 either, most local authorities are prepared to transfer the tenancy after divorce or separation, although they may require that certain conditions, e.g. as to payment of rent arrears, are fulfilled.

ii. *Property transfer order*

The second relevant statutory provision is s.24 Matrimonial Causes Act 1973. This enables a court, on or after granting a decree of divorce, nullity or judicial separation, to order one spouse to transfer specified property to the other. The essence of property, however, is transferability, hence a statutory tenancy, being of a personal nature, is outside this provision (*Hale* v. *Hale*, *The Times* 25th February 1975). And it has been doubted whether a council tenancy, whether or not property, would be an appropriate subject for a s.24 order (*Brent* v. *Brent* [1974] 2 All E.R. 1211).

c. Co-habitees

i. *The common law*

The provisions of the M.H.A. 1967 and the M.C.A. 1973, and the common-law obligations of a husband, e.g. to provide his wife with a home, apply only within the context of a proper marriage. Those who live together without marrying, even though they live as husband and wife and may have children, are not protected by this body of law. Such rights and obligations as either party has in relation to the common home must be sought outside matrimonial law.

If the couple are joint tenants each will have a right of occupation which can be protected, if necessary, by injunction. If, as is often the case, one party is merely the licensee of the other, that party has no sufficient proprietary interest to be protected by injunction, and so, in strict law, can be turned out at short notice. Even in the less likely event of the licence being contractual, no injunction would issue that would have the effect of forcing the parties to live together.

ii. *Recent developments in equity*

It has recently been decided, however, in two decisions of the Court of Appeal, that a co-habitee may be the beneficiary of a constructive trust over the common home, even though she has no rights at common law. In both *Eves* v. *Eves*, *The Times* 29th April 1975, and *Tanner* v. *Tanner*, *The Times* 3rd May 1975, a house was bought by the man on the understanding that it was to provide a home for himself, the woman, and their children. In *Eves*, the Court of Appeal ruled that the woman was entitled to a quarter share of its value. She had done a considerable amount of work on the house but had not put up any money. In *Tanner*, it was decided that the woman could not be required to leave the house after the relationship had ended. This decision appears to rest on the fact that the woman had been induced to believe that the house had been acquired as a joint home, rather than on the fact of work or money contributed by her. The general principle is stated by LORD DIPLOCK in *Gissing* v. *Gissing* [1971] A.C. 886 at p. 905: a constructive trust arises 'whenever the trustee has so conducted himself that it would be inequitable to allow him to deny to the *cestui que trust* a beneficial interest in the land acquired' (see also *Cooke* v. *Head* [1972] 1 W.L.R. 518 (C.A.)). *Tanner's* case is the widest application of this principle thus far.

It remains to be seen whether this extension of the equitable doctrine will reach all tenancies. Would it apply, for example, to a council or statutory tenancy, either of which is, arguably, not a proprietary interest?

iii. *Abandonment*

If the tenant abandons the other co-habitee, leaving him or her in occupation of the rented premises, the deserted party has no right to a transference of the tenancy. Nor does the continued occupation of the dwelling count as technical residence by the tenant under s.3(1)(*a*) R.A. 1968, if he has given up the intention to live there (*Smith (Colin) Music Ltd* v. *Ridge* [1975] 1 All E.R. 290 (C.A.)).

iv. *Succession*

A co-habitee can, however, succeed to a protected or statutory tenancy under s.3(1)(*b*) R.A. 1968 as a member of a deceased tenant's family, if there are children of the union (*Hawes* v. *Evenden* [1953] 2 All E.R. 737 (C.A.)).

CHAPTER 9

HARASSMENT, UNLAWFUL EVICTION, AND QUIET ENJOYMENT

1. Harassment

a. Generally

In conditions of housing stress, friction and ill-feeling are often engendered between a landlord and his tenant or lodger, particularly when they are sharing the same premises. In certain circumstances, the behaviour of the landlord (or anyone else, for that matter) towards the occupant will constitute the criminal offence of harassment, although it is not a crime for the occupant to harass the landlord.

This offence was introduced by s.30(2) Rent Act 1965, in the hope that it would discourage landlords from maliciously interfering with the rights and comfort of their tenants: (Report of the Committee on Housing in Greater London (1965) Cmnd 2605 p. 178).

It is not clear that this hope has been realised. The trivial and declining number of prosecutions brought under s.30(2) suggests that local authorities (to whom falls the task of prosecuting for harassment) prefer to keep criminal proceedings as a last resort, working instead through conciliatory agencies such as their harassment officer or tenant relations officer. Furthermore, the relatively slight penalties imposed on those who are convicted might suggest that, in many cases, the fault is not wholly with the landlord, who may simply have reacted to a bad tenant.

b. The meaning of harassment

In the last resort, however, the complexity of the definition of the offence is itself a discouragement to those who might wish to institute proceedings. Section 30(2) provides that it is an offence if, with intent to cause the residential occupier of any premises, *either* to give up occupation of all or part of the premises; *or* to refrain from exercising any right or pursuing any remedy in respect of the premises or any part of them, any person *either* does acts calculated to interfere with the peace or comfort of the residential occupier or members of his household; *or* persistently withdraws or withholds services which are reasonably required for the occupation of the premises as a residence.

c. Penalties

An offender is liable on summary conviction to a fine of up to £400 or imprisonment for a maximum of six months, or both, and if convicted on indictment, to an unlimited fine, or a maximum of two years' imprisonment, or both. These penalties apply both to a first and a subsequent conviction (s.30(3) R.A. 1965, as amended by s.30 of the Criminal Justice Act 1967).

d. The offender

The offence may be committed by anyone. Thus, in addition to the common case of a landlord harassing his tenant, it is possible for one occupant to harass another, or for one neighbour to harass another.

e. The victim

The offence of harassment is committed against the residential occupier or members of his household. A residential occupier is defined in s.30(5) R.A. 1965 as a person who occupies the premises as a residence, whether under a contract or by virtue of any enactment or rule of law which gives him the right to remain in occupation or restricts the right of any other person to recover possession of the premises.

This appears to cover the following categories of occupant:

(*a*) both protected and unprotected tenants; no tenant

can be dispossessed against his will without a court order, even if he is holding over after the expiry of a valid notice to quit (s.32 R.A. 1965, s.10 R.A. 1968).

(*b*) Licensees; it is a breach of contract to dispossess a contractual licensee; contrary to s.32 R.A. 1965 to evict a former service licensee who is holding over, and an offence under the Statute of Forcible Entry 1381 to dispossess by force anyone who has established himself in possession of land or premises. But if the owner manages to dispossess the erstwhile licensee without using force, e.g. by changing the locks on a dwelling while the occupant is out, the position is unclear.

(*c*) Squatters; if it is conceded that squatters are entitled to the protection of the Forcible Entry legislation (*contra* LORD DENNING M.R. in *McPhail* v. *Persons Unknown* above, p. 80) then they are in a similar position to former licensees who hold over.

(*d*) Owner-occupiers; in *Norton* v. *Knowles* [1969] 1 Q.B. 572 (D.C.) SALMON L.J. accepted a submission that s.30 Rent Act 1965 has no application to a freeholder occupying his own home, although there seems no reason in principle why such an occupier should not be protected.

The definition of a residential occupier does not comprehend the landlord as such. A recommendation of the Francis Committee (above, p. 93) on the Rent Acts, that the offence of harassment should be extended so as to protect landlords when exercising their rights over the demised premises, has yet to be implemented.

f. The prosecutor

It is the policy of police forces throughout the country not to institute prosecutions for harassment. This policy has been maintained since the offence was first introduced, and has the apparent approval of the central government (Francis Report above, p. 93, at p. 111). It is based upon a reluctance to enter into the complex, and essentially civil, law of landlord and tenant (but see *R.* v. *Commissioner of Police of the Metropolis, ex parte Blackburn* [1968] 2 Q.B. 118, especially *per* LORD DENNING M.R. at p. 136 (C.A.)).

The local authority is therefore deemed to be the appropriate prosecuting agency, although there is nothing in the Rent Act 1968 to prevent a private individual from prosecuting.

g. The mental element of the offence

It is not sufficient to show that the accused was motivated by some general malice or ill-feeling towards the residential occupier. It must be shown that he wished to induce him to give up his occupation of at least a part of the premises, or to desist from exercising some right over the premises or pursuing some remedy in respect of them. In practice local authorities have experienced considerable difficulty in establishing the mental element of harassment. In only a few cases will the landlord's behaviour be so unequivocal as to speak for itself.

h. The punishable behaviour

It seems, from the wording of s.30(2), that the offence is only committed if there is more than one act, unless the single action results in the persistent withdrawal or persistent withholding of services which are reasonably required for the occupation of the premises as a residence, as where the electricity supply is cut off by the landlord and not restored.

Because s.30(2) specifies acts, and not conduct, it is open to question whether the offence can be committed by words alone, e.g. by abuse or threats of eviction. It is also questionable whether it can be committed by a wrongful *omission*, e.g, by failing to repair, or by refusing to pay an electricity bill as a result of which the electricity board discontinues the supply. Since this is a criminal provision, and must therefore be interpreted restrictively, it would seem that a person does not 'withhold' or 'withdraw' a service if in fact he causes a third party to withhold or withdraw it. However, the element of persistence *is* supplied by a single withdrawal or withholding of a service which is not then restored. Nevertheless, it must be made clear in the information or indictment that the service was withheld or withdrawn beyond the day on which it was first terminated.

Nor is it clear whether the phrase 'calculated to interfere' signifies a further mental element, or whether it simply indicates a degree of likelihood. At all events, the allegation that the defendant's behaviour was calculated to interfere with the peace or comfort of the residential occupier is material to the offence, and so must not be omitted from the information or indictment (see generally *Westminster City Council* v. *Peart* (1968) 66 L.G.R. 561).

The Francis Committee (above, p. 93) lists the following actual instances as apparently valid examples of harassment:

(*a*) tenant temporarily bolted out (permanent exclusion would be unlawful eviction).
(*b*) essential services turned off;
(*c*) landlord assaulting tenant with knives;
(*d*) landlord taking up floorboards every weekend on the pretext of doing electrical wiring;
(*e*) taking slates off the roof to let the rain in;
(*f*) throwing petrol bombs through the letter box.

Only (*b*) and (*d*) are clear cases however. The rest are all questionable if they were single instances, and (*a*) and (*e*), which are examples of a single action with an enduring effect, cannot be said to amount to the persistent withdrawal of a service.

2. Unlawful eviction

a. The offence

This is an analogous offence to harassment, and carries the

same penalties. It was introduced, as a temporary measure, in the Protection From Eviction Act 1964, and is now to be found in s.30(1) Rent Act 1965. This makes it an offence for anyone unlawfully to deprive a residential occupier of any premises of his occupation of those premises or any part of them, or to attempt to do so. It is a defence to show a belief, entertained with reasonable cause, that the residential occupier had ceased to reside in the premises.

Since the offence is committed only if the eviction is unlawful, it will presumably not be committed if an occupant whose only protection is the Statute of Forcible Entry 1381 (e.g. an erstwhile licensee, other than a service licensee to whom s.32 R.A. 1965 applies, holding over) is *peaceably* deprived of his possession.

b. The meaning of 'premises'

A single room can constitute premises (*Thurrock U.D.C.* v. *Shina*, above, p. 98). It is not clear, however, whether the word extends to shared accommodation. If, for example, a tenant or lodger has exclusive possession of a bedsitting room, but shares a bathroom, is the offence of unlawful eviction committed by preventing him from using the bathroom? In *Shina's* case, LORD WIDGERY C.J. said, in relation to s.30(1) Rent Act 1965, that the word 'premises' must be given 'its normal wide meaning'; it is possible that this stops short of shared accommodation.

3. QUIET ENJOYMENT

A covenant (or condition) of quiet enjoyment is implied into a lease or an agreement for a lease by the common law. The scope of this obligation is variable: an express undertaking in the lease or agreement will circumscribe the limits of the landlord's obligation (*Miller* v. *Emcer Products Ltd* [1956] Ch. 304 (C.A.)). In all other cases it is established that the implied obligation does not extend to the actions of anyone claiming the premises under a paramount title to that of the landlord (*Jones* v. *Lavington* [1903] 1 K.B. 253 (C.A.)).

The covenant of quiet enjoyment has been said to represent a qualified protection for the tenant against interference with his peaceful possession and enjoyment of the premises by the landlord or anyone claiming through or under the landlord (*per* PEARSON L.J. in *Kenny* v. *Preen* [1963] 1 Q.B. 499 at p. 511 (C.A.)). Although a mere denial of the tenant's right to occupy is not a breach of this obligation (at least where the landlord believes in what he is saying) any unjustified physical interference, or threats of physical interference, e.g. a threat of forcible eviction, is a breach. Thus, instances of harassment will also supply examples of violations of the covenant of quiet enjoyment, e.g. cutting off main supplies is both harassment (*Peart's* case, above, p. 144) and contrary to the implied obligation (*Perera* v. *Vandiyar* [1952] 1 W.L.R. 672 (C.A.)).

It is not clear whether a breach of the covenant is committed if the landlord tricks the tenant into giving up possession, e.g. by the false offer of alternative accommodation, but there is reason to suppose that it is (see *Mafo* v. *Adams* [1970] 1 Q.B. 548 (C.A.)).

CHAPTER 10

RENT ALLOWANCES AND REBATES

It is beyond the scope of this book to examine the complex provisions governing the rent which a landlord may legitimately charge for particular premises, but a brief outline of local authority rent rebate and allowance schemes seems in order and is given in this chapter. A detailed examination of both these topics can be found in T. M. Aldridge, *Rent Control and Leasehold Enfranchisement*, 6th Edn, Oyez Publishing Limited.

1. Duty to operate rebate and allowance schemes

The Housing Finance Act 1972 imposes a duty upon housing authorities to operate a scheme for making rebates from Housing Revenue Account rents (i.e. rents received in respect of premises provided under Part V H.A. 1957), and for providing allowances towards private rents in certain defined circumstances. The philosophy behind this provision is expressed in D. of E. Circular 154/73 para. 2: 'local authorities are responsible for helping all tenants in their area who are unable to afford the rent of accommodation suited to their needs'.

The Greater London Council, however, is not obliged to operate a scheme, since the G.L.C. is not considered a local authority for this purpose (s.19(11) H.F.A. 1972).

2. Nature of schemes

The rebate schemes must follow the lines of a model scheme set out in the Third Schedule to the 1972 Act, from which an authority may deviate only within fairly strict limits; it cannot grant a smaller allowance or rebate than would have been payable or deductible under the model scheme, nor can the total amount of rebates or allowances exceed the permitted maximum. The permitted maximum is 110 per cent of the amount which would have been granted had the authority operated the statutory model scheme (ss.22(1), 20(8) H.F.A. 1972).

3. Publication of schemes

Copies of the housing or local authority's particular rebate or allowance scheme must be made available for public inspection at the authority's principal office at all reasonable times and free of charge (s.24(1) H.F.A. 1972). In addition, any *private* landlord who grants a new tenancy after 1st January 1973 must give his tenant written particulars of the local authority's rent allowance scheme. Wilful failure or refusal to do so is a summary offence, punishable by a maximum fine of £50. Any rent book or similar document issued to a tenant whose rent is payable weekly must also contain these particulars (s.20(10), (11) and (12)).

4. Eligibility

a. Council tenants

Anyone who occupies a Housing Revenue Account dwelling as his home may apply for a rent rebate (i.e. a deduction from his council rent) unless:

(*a*) a substantial proportion of the rent is attributable to the use of furniture; in fact relatively few Housing Revenue Account dwellings are let furnished, but in such a case the tenant may in any event qualify for a rent *allowance*, as if he were a private tenant (s.19(8A) H.F.A. 1972; below, p. 149); or

(*b*) he is a service tenant; or

(*c*) the premises are let partly (or wholly) for business purposes (s.18(3) H.F.A. 1972).

A person in receipt of supplementary benefit does not, however, qualify in any circumstances.

b. Private tenants

Rent allowances, i.e. cash grants to help meet private rents, may be payable to private residential tenants. A private tenant for this purpose means:

(*a*) a protected or statutory tenant, as those terms are defined in the Rent Act 1968 (above, pp. 108–18); or

(*b*) one who occupies a dwelling under a Part VI contract (above, pp. 96–100) or who would do so but for the fact that a substantial part of his rent is fairly attributable to the provision of board (s.19(4) H.F.A. 1972); or

(*c*) a person who would be a protected tenant, but for the fact that his landlord is one of the following: the Crown; a *county* council; the Housing Corporation; a registered housing association or a housing trust within the meaning of s.5 Rent Act 1968.

The tenancy must be wholly residential, however, and, as in the case of rebates, no rent allowance is payable to a person in receipt of supplementary benefit.

c. Persons treated as private tenants

A local authority *may* treat as a private tenant anyone who occupies a local authority dwelling which is not a Housing Revenue Account dwelling, if that person would have been entitled to a rent rebate had he been occupying such a dwelling. Furthermore, a person *must* be treated as a private tenant if he occupies a furnished Housing Revenue Account dwelling and a substantial proportion of the rent is properly attributable to the use of furniture and he is therefore disqualified from applying for a rent *rebate* (s.19(11) H.F.A. 1972).

5. Quantification of rebates

The amount of rebate or allowance is computed according to the complicated formulae of the Third Schedule to the Housing Finance Act 1972. The relevant factors are:

(*a*) the number of persons residing in the rented accommodation, any sub-tenants apart. Generally speaking, the rebate or allowance will increase according to the number of dependent children in the house and decrease according to the number of non-dependants who live there. A non-dependant is anyone residing in the dwelling other than the tenant, a spouse, and dependent children. 'Spouse' signifies a person who is actually living with the tenant in the relationship of man and wife, and not a person who is married to, but living apart from, the tenant;

(*b*) the income of the tenant and any spouse, adjusted by reference to a number of specified factors (Sched. 3, para. 9 H.F.A. 1972): and

(*c*) the rent, adjusted by reference to a number of specified factors (s.25 H.F.A. 1972).

Rebates and allowances will not be made above a certain maximum or below a certain minimum figure. In order to determine entitlement or to calculate the amount of rebate or allowance, the authority is empowered to call for detailed information as to the persons who live in the dwelling, and as to the income of the tenant and his spouse.

It is, of course, an offence under the general law of theft if a tenant illegally obtains more than his due under a rebate or allowance scheme.

INDEX